How to Win at Aptitude Tests

The job's already mine, old man?!

How to Win at Aptitude Tests

Paul Pelshenke

Translated from the German by
Jill Sutcliffe

Thorsons
An Imprint of HarperCollins*Publishers*

Thorsons
An Imprint of HarperCollins*Publishers*
77–85 Fulham Palace Road,
Hammersmith, London W6 8JB
1160 Battery Street,
San Francisco, California 94111-1213

Published by Thorsons 1993
10 9 8 7 6 5 4 3 2

A catalogue record for this book
is available from the British Library

ISBN 0 7225 2814 0

Phototypeset by Harper Phototypesetters Limited,
Northampton, England
Printed in Great Britain by
HarperCollinsManufacturing Glasgow

Contents

Introduction

by Paul Kline, PhD DSc, Professor of Psychometrics at the University of Exeter

A few years ago when the economy was booming there was a shortage of trained personnel. There were more jobs than applicants. This meant that to attract employees, employers had to offer excellent training opportunities and conditions of work.

All this has changed with the European recession: it is difficult to obtain a job. Unemployment is high. Employers can demand better and better qualifications and set stiffer and stiffer tests. All this creates great difficulties for young people trying to get a job. Many of them have been unable to find jobs even after several years and begin to lose hope. All this is bad for society generally and particularly for the unemployed.

Nevertheless, the passive acceptance of this dismal fate, blaming politicians or educationalists or capitalists, for example, is useless. A proper appraisal of business and commerce shows that there *are* jobs available but that for each one there is severe competition. Applicants must sell themselves and demonstrate that they are best for the job. From the viewpoint of the employer, it is necessary to pick the best candidates.

This selection process is difficult, since, for most jobs, a variety of characteristics, knowledge, special abilities and personal qualities, such as friendliness or toughness, for example, are required and employers have to assess them. However, school reports and even examination results are often insufficient for this purpose. Where examinations have been set and marked by schools, results may not be comparable and different examination boards may have different syllabuses. New and traditional maths are good examples of this. As a result employers have turned to objective aptitude testing, as is used in the USA.

The principles of aptitude testing for selection are straightforward enough. Employers make careful job analyses of exactly what is required for any job and then use aptitude tests to measure the necessary characteristics. Typical aptitide tests measure intelligence, verbal ability, perseverance at tedious tasks, logical thinking, spatial ability, and general problem solving. More specific ability tests, which might be required for a particular job can also be developed. Such tests are usually constructed by psychologists who specialise in testing and who are known as psychometrists.

Generally conventional school education, even despite the recent emphasis on testing, is not a good preparation for taking objective aptitude or psychological tests. These require applicants to work fast and on their own and to be generally competitive. Their multiple choice answers are very different from the essays which are often required at school.

This book aims to train people to do their best at objective psychological tests of all kinds which are used in the selection process. It offers a set of training programmes which people can do on their own, in their own time. The users of this book should stick closely to the programme, going carefully through the test items, observing the time limits, and checking their results in the answers section of the book.

While it is sensible for candidates to concentrate on those tests which seem most relevant to the jobs they would like to do, it is also useful to do the other tests. This is because many employers may decide to assess more than the bare minimum required.

These practice tests are not taken from actual aptitude

tests, of which there are enormous numbers. This would not be ethical or even useful. Rather, they are designed to give confidence in taking all kinds of tests, so that when the actual selection tests have to be taken it all seems familiar and you can give your best performance.

There is nothing unfair in carefully preparing for a test and acquainting yourself with what is required. On the contrary, it is what any sensible person would do if he or she could. In the past such preparation was almost impossible. This book makes it possible.

Plan for the Practice Section

The practical exercises are intended for training. In the actual examinations each complete aptitude test is timed, and the timing is very tight. It is hardly ever possible to complete the sub-tests and to do them correctly in the prescribed time. The number of questions completed will differ, helping to identify the best performances.

As it is primarily a matter of familiarising yourself with the test requirements at this stage, you need not be concerned with working to time. Confidence and speed come, as everyone knows, with practice and familiarity.

In the main, three areas of skill and knowledge are examined in these tests, even though the division of these areas may sometimes appear pedantic and artificial.

1 Intelligence, the capacity to do the correct and appropriate thing in new, unexpected situations.

We use so-called one-dimensional intelligence tests ('intelligence-structure tests') and ask the examinee to:

- continue numerical series
- find and create patterns
- recognise similarities/odd-ones-out/differences
- form analogies (relationships of one thing to another)
- establish logical consistency
- develop and demonstrate an ability to observe and remember.

2 Section relevant to work

This is where the examinee's speed, accuracy, methodical organisation, concentration, resistance to stress, and perseverance are assessed. The sub-tests are:

- identifying specific symbols
- identifying errors in copying
- comparing addresses
- putting letters in order
- calculating efficiently
- accuracy and organisation
- technical understanding.

3 General knowledge and school subjects

For this it is important for the examinee to have solid but not special knowledge of how to write correctly and do simple arithmetic as well as having technical know-how and awareness of technical processes. So-called general knowledge will be assessed first. It is difficult to plan preparation for this because a great variety of areas such as culture, history, geography, biology, politics, commerce, current affairs, or suchlike could be drawn upon. Frequently, also, essays are asked for. The vast subject of essay-writing is of course outside the scope of this book. Nearly everyone must have had their fill of writing essays – and yet here too you have to be prepared for new (test-) situations. The most demanding examiner also knows that no one can be a specialist in everything, and therefore no substantial decisions are likely to be based on your performance here.

You are recommended, however, to be well informed about current affairs (political and economic), as well as recent British history. The subject areas here are:

- general knowledge
- school subjects generally
- spelling
- mathematical reasoning
- arithmetic
- geometry.

Practice Section

Intelligence section

1 *Continuing a series of numbers*

Series of numbers are given which have to be continued, mostly with one number (but occasionally with two numbers). First, you have to discover the pattern and progression of the series. To do this, it is helpful to write the working numbers for your solution (e.g. +1 +2 +3 . . .) into the series of numbers given (see the example below). Using this system, once you have found the pattern you will discover the missing number(s).

1st exercise example

1   4   10   16   19   25   31   ?

The numbers increase, so addition and/or multiplication are involved.

Working out and solution:

$1_{+3}4_{+6}10_{+6}16_{+3}19_{+6}25_{+6}31_{+3}\mathbf{34}$

2nd exercise example

8   4   16   8   32   16   64   ?

The numbers become alternatively smaller and bigger, so what is involved is successively division/subtraction and/or addition/multiplication.

Working out and solution:

$$8 \;{}_{\div 2}\; 4 \;{}_{\times 4}\; 16 \;{}_{\div 2}\; 8 \;{}_{\times 4}\; 32 \;{}_{\div 2}\; 16 \;{}_{\times 4}\; 64 \;{}_{\div 2}\; 32$$

Number series requiring one number to be found

For practice, write the figures given below on a sheet of paper big enough to allow calculations alongside, and on this sheet try out different ways of solving the problem, if your method isn't right first time. Alternatively photocopy this page. In this way you can use the training units several times.

Exercise examples

1	1	2	4	8	16	32	64	______
2	1	2	6	24	120	720	5040	______
3	1	6	2	8	13	9	36	______
4	2	8	4	6	24	12	14	______
5	3	9	8	24	23	69	68	______
6	5	10	14	12	17	21	19	______
7	120	122	115	125	127	120	130	______
8	2	12	6	36	12	72	36	______
9	20	4	40	55	11	110	125	______
10	3	4	6	10	18	34	66	______

More commonly nowadays the results will be checked by the examiner by overlaying a stencil containing the correct answers. This is why you are asked to cross out the numbers which give the correct answer in a set of boxes that contain a numerical sequence. That makes the examiner's task of checking the answers easier and quicker, but it may on occasion confuse the examinee. Nevertheless, the way to break the code and establish the numerical order isn't changed by that.

Here are 3 examples:

1st example:

Numerical order

0 1 2 3 4 5 6 7 8 9

If the correct answer is 268, the right way of answering this is shown in the strip below.

0	1	~~2~~	3	4	5	~~6~~	7	~~8~~	9

2nd example:

Numerical progression

1 4 8 13 19 26 34 ?

The progression consists of increasing the number to be added by one each time, starting with the three, thus: +3/ +4/ +5 and so on, so that the solution is:

$$1_{+3}{}^{4}{}_{+4}{}^{8}{}_{+5}{}^{13}{}_{+6}{}^{19}{}_{+7}{}^{26}{}_{+8}{}^{34}{}_{+9}{}^{\mathbf{43}}$$

In the second example we find another strip of increasing numbers:

Numerical order

0	1	2	3	4	5	6	7	8	9

The correct answer should be 43, so cross out the figures three and four, even though the four in the answer precedes the three, but does not do so, however, in the strip below. The correct solution is therefore:

0	1	2	~~3~~	~~4~~	5	6	7	8	9

The figures in the strip are not always in rising numerical order from nought to nine. Individual numbers may be repeated or not included.

Numerical order

0	1	1	2	3	3	4	5	5	6

Solution giving 43

0	1	1	2	~~3~~	3	~~4~~	5	5	6

or
Numerical order

Solution giving 43

9	2	5	4	0	5	1	7	3	2

Example 3

9	2	5	~~4~~	0	5	1	7	~~3~~	2

Numerical Progression

1 6 12 17 34 39 78 ?

The progression is +5/×2/+5/×2 and so on, so that leads to the answer:

$$1 \xrightarrow{+5} 6 \xrightarrow{\times 2} 12 \xrightarrow{+5} 17 \xrightarrow{\times 2} 34 \xrightarrow{+5} 39 \xrightarrow{\times 2} 78 \xrightarrow{+5} \mathbf{83}$$

The result strip, with solution:

7	~~3~~	1	0	~~8~~	5	6	4	2	9

Further practice:

11	10	40	20	80	40	160	80	?
12	80	240	120	360	180	540	270	?

11 result strip

6	7	1	0	2	4	3	5	8	9

12 result strip

1	4	8	4	3	7	6	5	0	9

2 *Finding and establishing regular patterns*

In this, figures, letters or symbols are listed according to an ingenious system.

In order to identify the pattern, you have to begin a series sometimes on the left, sometimes on the right. Often you have to jump over symbols so that sometimes every second symbol – when put next to each other – produces a regular pattern.

When you have found the pattern, an intruder ('an odd-one-out') comes to light. This intruder has to be identified or corrected (or both).

Example 1

1 3 5 7 9 11 12 15

In the progression of odd numbers above, the 12 is wrong.

Answer:

13
1 3 5 7 9 11 ~~12~~ 15

Example 2

c W e T g R i P k

The small letters appear in alphabetical order from left to right, and you have to jump over a capital letter between each one. With the capital letters it is the other way round. The capital W is out of sequence.

Solution:

c W e T g R i P k

1	0	4	0	8	0	12	0	15	0
2	AA	h	BB	g	CC	f	EE	e	EE
3	2	4	8	16	32	16	12	4	2
4	63	55	49	42	35	28	21	14	7
5	5	GG	10	HH	15	EE	20	DD	25
6	k	l	M	n	o	P	q	r	s
7	1	2	4	7	12	16	22	29	37
8	1	4	3	6	5	4	7	10	9
9	III	6	IV	6	V	4	VI	3	VII
10	B	I	E	h	H	f	K	c	N
11	a	5	e	9	i	12	m	17	q
12	r	1	t	4	v	7	x	9	z

3 *Happy families and odd-ones-out*

Here we shall work with concepts (verbal) and symbols (non-verbal). Connections have to be made or found between concepts and between symbols. Odd-ones-out have to be eliminated.

Verbal examples:

1 What do Mallorca, Sardinia, Corsica and Rhodes have in common?

'Islands' is not enough. 'Mediterranean islands' is better. 'Mediterranean islands which belong to different European countries' is even better, and is what the examiner is looking for from a suitable candidate.

2 Make up a group of four, and identify the odd-one-out in the words rowan – beech – oak – spruce – lime. You have to find an appropriate common factor from which it will probably emerge why the odd-one-out is different. Thus:
rowan – beech – oak – lime are indigenous deciduous trees. As a conifer, spruce is different – even though it is also an indigenous tree.

Examples of symbols:

Here you have to be strictly logical, to think in abstract terms, and decide quickly. The problems set are unfamiliar for the inexperienced candidate. The results achieved will of course count highly with the examiner. As several aspects of intelligence will be tested at the same time by these sub-tests, extensive training practice is necessary at this point.

In general, in the series of exercises that follow, five symbols will be given, from among which the odd-one-out has to be discovered. When four symbols go together, the outsider can usually be quickly identified. It becomes more difficult when out of five symbols two symbols make a pair, so that the outsider can only be found after the pairs have been made up. In each case the odd-one-out has to be marked with a cross, with its identifying letter attached to the number of the exercise, so that combinations such as 3a or 5d result (which are of course incorrect answers here).

1 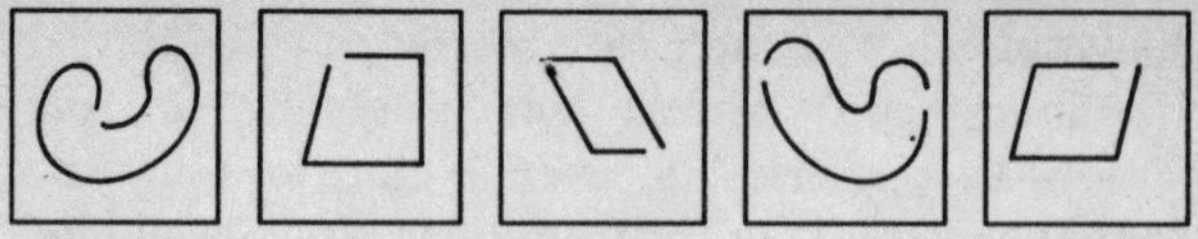

a b c d e

Answer 1d

Because symbol d is the only one that has two openings.

2 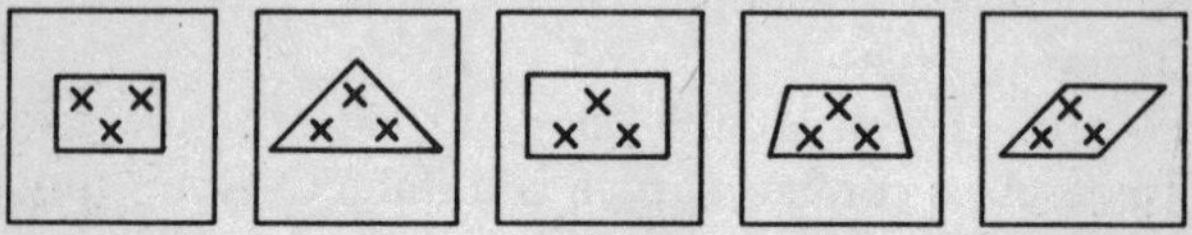

a b c d e

Answer 2a

Because the crosses are arranged differently from the others (2 above, 1 below).

3 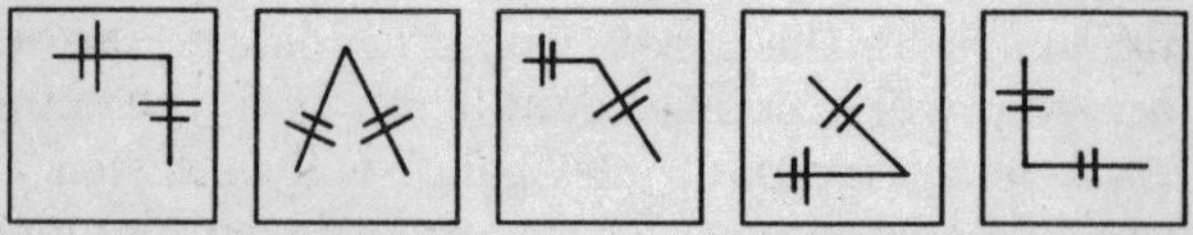

a b c d e

Answer 3c

Because a and e (right-angled) and b and d (acute angled) make pairs, so that c is the odd-one-out, being obtuse.

4 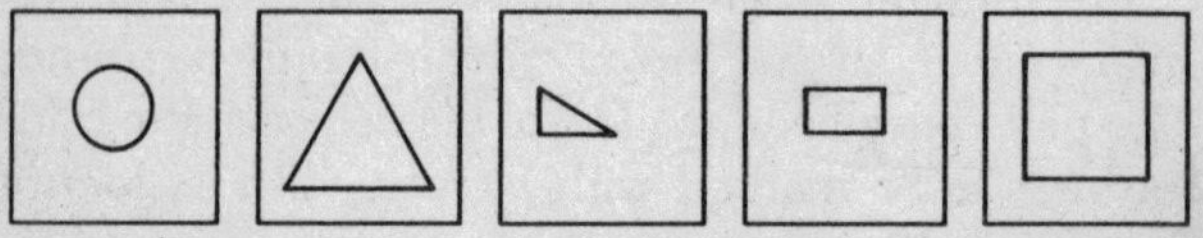

a b c d e

Answer 4a

Because b and e as well as c and d make pairs (same height), that leaves a, as it is in between the two sizes and, moreover, it is round.

Language

Verbal

1 In the list below are different animals. They are to be put into sensible groups of three. The groups should have as appropriate and definite a generic connection as possible.

lion	owl	canary
parrot	nightjar	rattlesnake
skylark	leopard	giraffe
adder	sparrow hawk	bat
carp	goose	cow
zebra	robin	buzzard
budgerigar	pig	eagle
seagull	elephant	shellfish
tiger	duck	sand-snake
horse	blackbird	herring

Possible answers

non-European beasts of prey
lion – leopard – tiger

exotic cagebirds
budgerigar – parrot – canary

indigenous – and non-European – water-fowl
duck – seagull – goose

indigenous – and non-European – farm animals
cow – horse – pig

European-based birds of prey
sparrow hawk – buzzard – eagle

indigenous song birds
blackbird – skylark – robin

poisonous crawling vertebrates – or poisonous snakes
adder – rattlesnake – sand-snake

large animals of the jungle or prairie
giraffe – zebra – elephant

locally catchable, edible fish
shellfish – carp – herring

indigenous night-flying creatures
owl – nightjar – bat

2 First make up groups of three.
Then find the appropriate generic term.

cedar	Manchester	Paris
Athens	Corsica	Avon
sycamore	scooter	hockey
Thames	biro	Jersey
London	bicycle	kidney
Crete	crayon	Rome
pencil	beech	volleyball
water polo	stone-pine	maple
liver	moped	Ouse
pine	intestines	Durham

3 Make up groups of five and give them generic names.

oak	Windrush	wood
Volga	Pennines	Rhine
wheat	cow	beech
maize	ash	Scots pine
South Downs	goat	peat

Amazon	oats	Tokyo
Nile	coal	Cotswolds
Vienna	fir	Athens
Madrid	juniper	Santiago
Chilterns	Severn	Rome
cedar	Paris	Thames
barley	Niger	birch
rye	sheep	sycamore
fuel-oil	Cape Town	briquette
spruce	Mersey	Avon
Washington	horse	donkey
Tehran	Mendips	Chilterns

4 Here are more sets of five to be put together. Each group should be in a sensible sequence. Indicate for each group what criteria are being used in establishing the sequence. Such criteria could be, for example: time, weight, distance, consistency, specific gravity, price, size, height, length, width, age, frequency.

hundredweight	teenager	kilogram
spring	ton	twenty
small town	nine	dog
small child	large town	beggar
scooter	cockchafer	twelve
seven	receiver of pocket-money	gram
rocket	horse	elephant
country	sea	rivulet
ant	e	employer
village	bicycle	motorbike
school-child	ounce	river
i	stream	infant
millionaire	continent	u
worker	a	adult
thirty	car	o

5 There is an odd-one-out among the six words in each row. The outsiders – according to test practice – are to be crossed out or identified with consecutive numbers (e.g. 1 stucco).

1 carpet – floor – linoleum – stucco – step on – soft
2 air – pollution – movement – drink – breathe – filter
3 travel – healthy – harvest – vitamin – meal – vegetables
4 damp – pour – rain – cool – quite – fall
5 homework – exercise-book – teacher – cabbage – certificate – learn
6 heat – harmless – extinguish – burn – fire – matches
7 paper – page – metal – title – read – prize
8 bark – coat – wolf down – pay attention – lead – cat
9 recover – work – holiday – travel – hotel – sleep soundly
10 line – hear – speak – see – number – telephone
11 apple – pear – plum – cherry – lemon – raspberry
12 potato – carrot – radish – turnip – onion – tomato
13 tooth – juice – drink – sip – fluid – thirst
14 see – hear – observe – learn – smell – travel
15 Christmas – celebrate – fir tree – winter – beach – candle
16 car – traffic light – driving licence – harbour – right of way – collide
17 transmitter – circuit-breaker – reception – programme – telephone – news
18 language – hear – astonishing – say – make a speech – hearing
19 write – observe – postage stamp – sender – address – read
20 dog – cat – hamster – sparrow – budgerigar – canary

Symbols

1

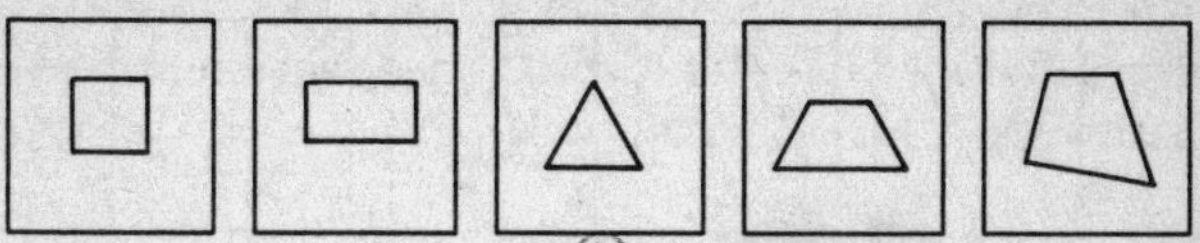

a b c d e

2

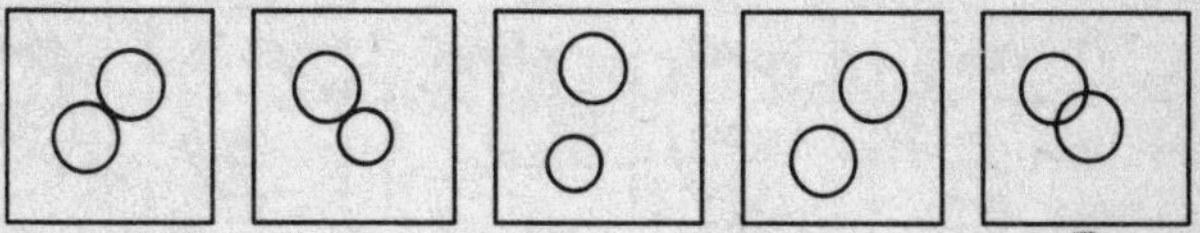

a b c d e

3

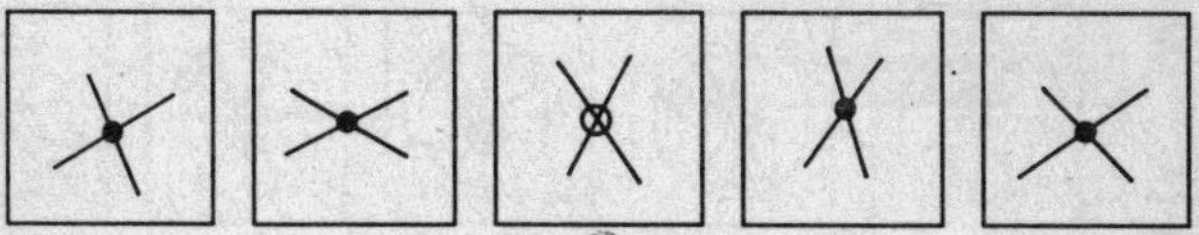

a b c d e

4

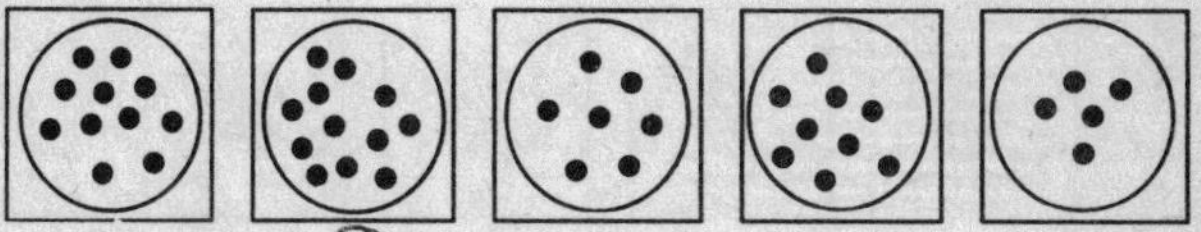

a b c d e

5

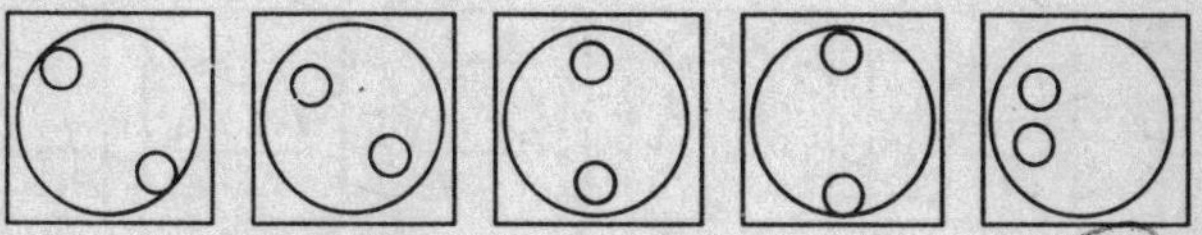

a b c d e

Symbols

6

a b c d e

7

a b c d e

8

a b c d e

9

a b c d e

10

a b c d e

Symbols

11

a b c d e

12

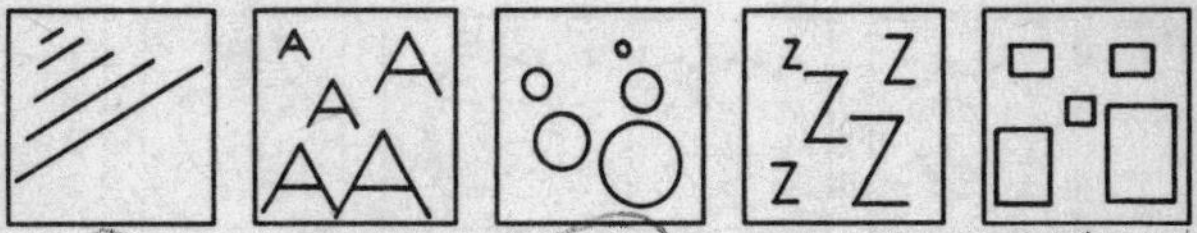

a b c d e

13

a b c d e

14

a b c d e

15

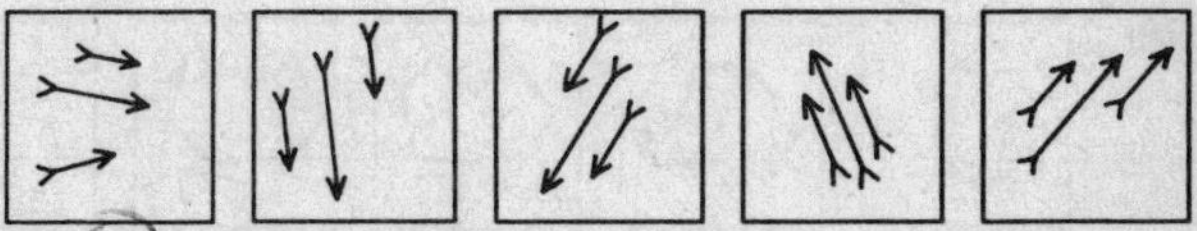

a b c d e

Symbols

16

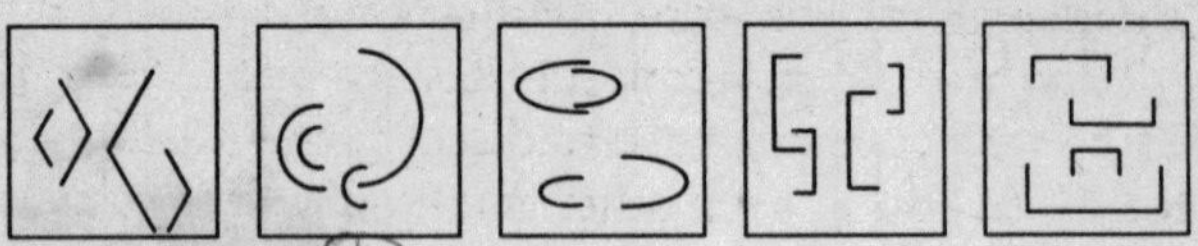

a b c d e

17

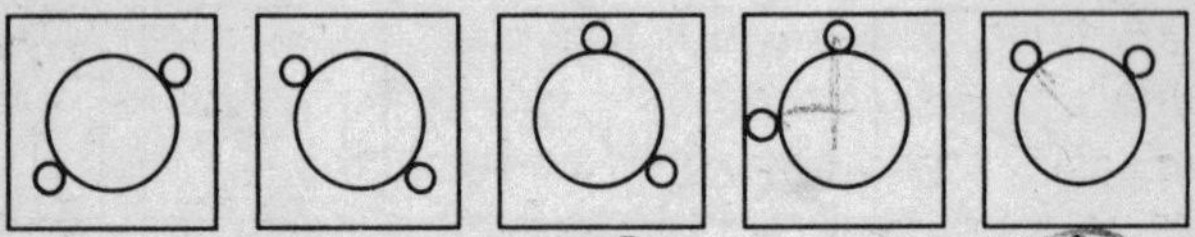

a b c d e

18

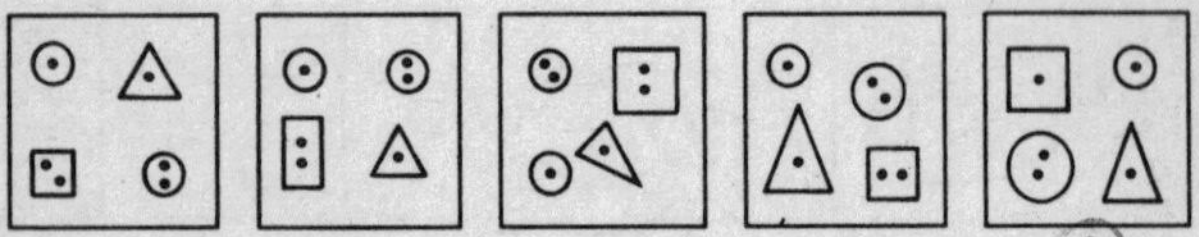

a b c d e

19

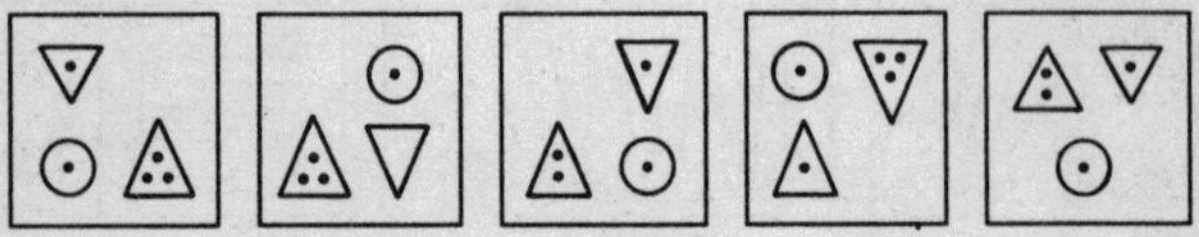

a b c d e

20

a b c d e

4 *Forming analogies*

Analogous means corresponding to or similar to.

To form analogies, concepts have to be linked in pairs. To do this, first you have to discover the relationship of the given pair to each other, so that the second pair can be related in the same way.

Here you are most likely to come across recurring basic types such as causes, consequences, raw materials, products of, foodstuffs, defences, tools, parts of something, parts of the body, means of transport, units of measurement, opposites, and so on.

As a first step towards solving the problem, link the given concepts in the form 'A is to B', in order to narrow it down to a precise criterion, like, for example, 'is produced from'.

Examples

1 paper: wood = ____________ : skin
Paper is produced from wood, or wood is the raw material for paper.
Answer: leather (paper is related to wood as leather is to skin).

2 runners: ____________ = ____________ : car
Sledges move on runners, cars on wheels.
Answer: runners: sledges = wheels: car(s)

3 music: note = word: ____________
a) phrase b) communication c) writing d) letter
When there is a multiple choice the appropriate concept must be selected (in this case: letter).
Answer: 3(d) because music is written in notes, words in letters.

4 iron: ore = ____________ : ____________
a) thunder : lightning b) butter : milk
c) house : foundations d) interest : loan
The pairs suggested – (a)-(d) – are at first sight similar to the pair above, iron : ore, but only butter : milk fits the criterion (or: 'is produced from').
Answer: 4(b) because butter is produced from milk.

Forming analogies

1 1 fish : ____________ = sheep : bone
2 fish : scale = bird : ____________
3 bird : ____________ = dog : muzzle
4 horse : hoof = ____________ : foot
5 ____________ : budgerigar = kennel : dog
6 hedgehog : spines = tortoise : ____________
7 songbird : insects = ____________ : grass
8 bricklayer : ____________ = artist : fee

2 1 night : day = ____________ : light
2 fire : water = thirst : ____________
3 happiness : sadness = ____________ : defeat
4 rails : railway = street : ____________
5 Spain : peseta = ____________ : dollar
6 professor : student = teacher : ____________
7 daughter : mother = ____________ : father
8 noise : ear = smell : ____________

3 1 all : nothing = many : ____________
a) everywhere b) nowhere c) few d) often
2 anger : display of temper = joke: ____________
a) punchline b) laughter c) reserved table
d) carnival
3 Commandment : religion = law : ____________
a) justice b) paragraph c) patrol d) police
4 painter : paintbrush = blacksmith : ____________
a) anvil b) iron c) fire d) hammer

5 bread : grain = cognac : _____ WINE _____
a) alcohol b) France c) bottle d) wine
6 kilometre : metre = centimetre : _____ c _____
a) yardstick b) length c) millimetre d) decimetre
7 metre : length = kilogramme : _____ B _____
a) hundredweight b) weight c) scales
d) measurement
8 heating : warmth = refrigerator : _____ d _____
a) food b) river c) aggregate d) coldness

4 1 filament : lightbulb = _____ d _____ : candle
a) wax b) light c) fire d) wick
2 cigarette : smoke = _____ a _____ : steam
a) water b) heat c) evaporation d) chimney
3 water : wave = _____ B _____ : wind
a) storm b) movement c) sail d) air
4 root : plant = ____________ : dog
a) tail b) nose c) coat d) ear
5 stallion : mare = _____ d _____ : hen
a) egg b) soup c) feather d) cockerel
6 corkscrew : bottle = _____ room _____ : door
a) knob b) hinge c) wood d) room
7 head-teacher : school = _____ b _____ : office
a) desk b) manager c) firm d) telephone
8 ox : steak = _____ c _____ : egg
a) shoe b) skin c) hen d) saddler

5 1 person : shoes = d
a) elephant : trunk
b) cat : claw
c) fish : fin
d) horse : horseshoe

2 cowboy : jeans = b
a) bishop : mitre
b) fitter : overalls
c) gardener : spade
d) grandmother : reading glasses

3 engineer : drawing board =
a) locksmith : vice
b) farmer : agriculture
c) inventor : idea
d) bride : ring

4 head-teacher : teacher =
a) shop-steward : employee
b) bus-driver = passenger
c) company : shareholder
d) inspector : head-teacher

5 Germany : USA =
a) Israel : Jordan
b) Peru : S. America
c) Madrid : Spain
d) (former) East Germany : (former) USSR

6 rudder : ship =
a) brand-name : motorbike
b) brake : car
c) lamp : bicycle
d) joystick: aeroplane

7 brother : sister =
a) age : youth
b) aunt : cousin
c) boy : girl
d) uncle : nephew

8 England : Yorkshire =
a) The Alps : mountains
b) Heathrow : airport
c) USA : Texas
d) North Sea : harbour

6 1 banister : stairs =
a) rung : ladder
b) key : key-hole
c) window : room
d) rail : ship

2 youth hostel : hiker =
a) stadium : athlete
b) hotel : holiday-maker
c) cinema : audience
d) cathedral : Christ

3 fir : cone =

a) tree : branch
b) cactus : spine
c) palm : date
d) cherry : juice

4 ocean : water =

a) desert : sand
b) sea : ship
c) ship : sail
d) beach : holiday

5 plastics : mineral oil =

a) petrol : diesel oil
b) natural gas : fuel oil
c) tar : coal
d) kiln : briquette

6 crime : punishment =

a) prison : warder
b) tournament : umpire
c) police : arrest
d) depression : rain

7 paper : scissors =

a) sheet of paper : envelope
b) wood : saw
c) uranium : nuclear power
d) nail : hammer

8 record : music =

a) book : text
b) radio : broadcast
c) tape recorder : head
d) telephone : cable

7 1 Human being : intelligence =

a) cause : mood
b) dog : game bird
c) vibration : note
d) animal : instinct

2 binder : documents =

a) building site : noise
b) bill : receipt
c) till : money
d) church : parish

3 plot of land : fence =

a) picture : frame
b) chicken : bone
c) finger : joint
d) garden : border

4 fire : water =

a) snow : rain
b) ice : water
c) heat : thirst
d) hunger : eating

5 noise : ear =

a) bang : explosion
b) taste : tongue
c) head-cold : nose
d) pain : illness

6 head : brain =

a) intelligence : thought
b) religion : belief
c) bone : marrow
d) knee : joint

7 tension : relaxation =

a) start : aim
b) stress : calmness
c) holiday : departure
d) music : speech

8 earthquake : collapse =

a) call : hear
b) morning : evening
c) sun : rain
d) tidal wave : flooding

8 Several analogous groupings are possible here, e.g.:

____________ : cage = ____________ : house

Examples of correct answers:

bird : cage = person : house
perch : cage = chair : house
sand : cage = carpet : house
wire : cage = walls : house

Although the possibility of choice in the above answers (multiple choice method) always provides a 25 per cent chance of a lucky hit, more thought is necessary. On the other hand, more ways of approaching the problem correctly are allowed (see examples above).

1 ____________ : tobacco = ____________ : brandy
2 ____________ : life = accident : ____________
3 bread : ____________ = raisin : ____________
4 spoke : ____________ = ____________ : reading glasses
5 ____________ : acid = bacon : ____________
6 chill : ____________ = short-circuit : ____________
7 ____________ : distance = ____________ : time
8 skates : ____________ = ____________ : asphalt

5 *Logical consistency and sequences*

Mostly these contain several symbols, numbers or letters in a logical sequence. First you have to recognise how the sequence is constructed and how it works. When you have discovered that, the row has to be completed with another symbol, or the same one. You will be shown several symbols from which to choose the logical one in the sequence (by checking them off).

Sometimes new concepts will be introduced which have to be inserted in a logical sequence. Criteria for these can be age, weight, size, price, distance, toughness, etc.

1 Example using symbols

1
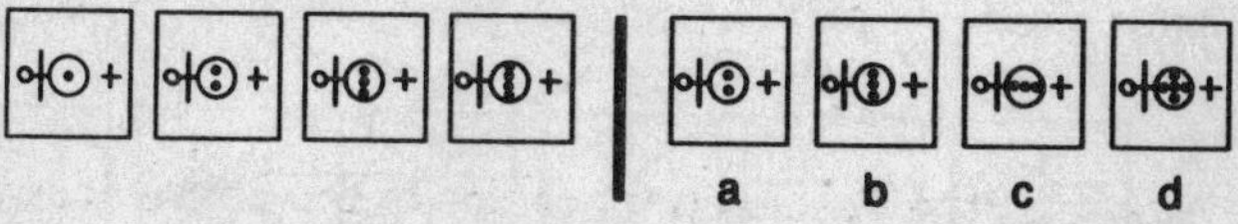

Answer: 1d, as there have to be 5 dots in the circle. (1st circle 1 dot; 2nd circle 2 dots; 3rd circle 3 dots; and so on.)

2 Example using concepts

a) marriage b) confirmation c) christening d) burial
Answer: c – b – a – d (chronological sequence)

3 Example using dots

1

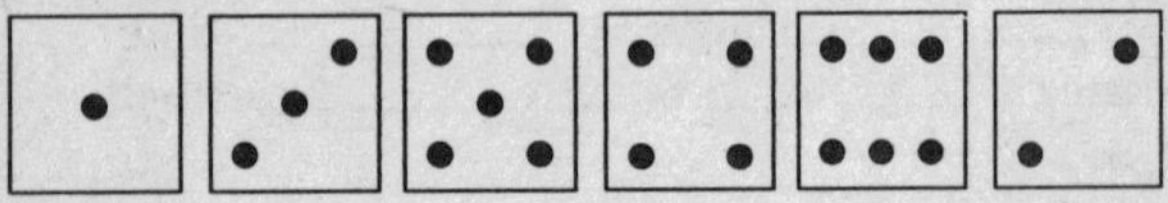

1	2	3	4	5	6

Answer: 1 – 6 – 2 – 4 – 3 – 5 (number of dots)

4 Example using letters

R	T	W	C	F	K
1	2	3	4	5	6

Answer: 4 – 5 – 6 – 1 – 2 – 3 (alphabetical order)

5 Example using number values

$1\frac{5}{7}$	$\frac{14}{8}$	1,81	$1\frac{3}{5}$	1,18	$\frac{17}{10}$
1	2	3	4	5	6

Answer: 5 – 4 – 6 – 1 – 2 – 3 (order of size, ascertainable by determining the decimal value)

Establish logical sequences

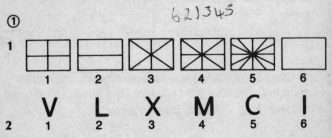

621345

①

1

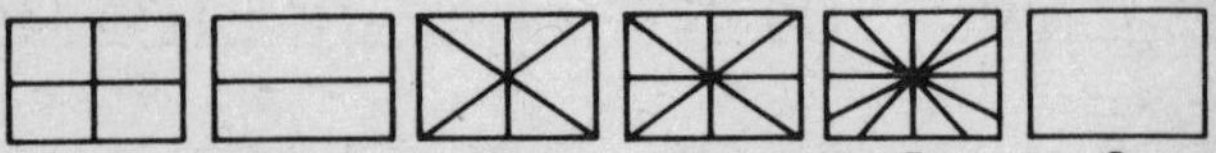

1	2	3	4	5	6

2

V	L	X	M	C	I
1	2	3	4	5	6

 613254

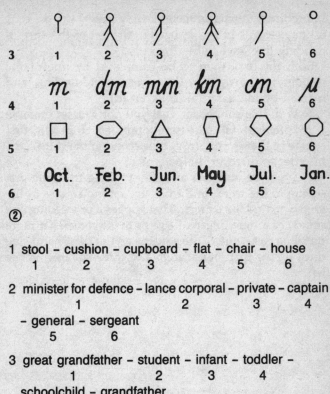

3 1 2 3 4 5 6

m dm mm km cm µ

4 1 2 3 4 5 6

5 1 2 3 4 5 6

Oct. Feb. Jun. May Jul. Jan.

6 1 2 3 4 5 6

②

1 stool – cushion – cupboard – flat – chair – house
1 2 3 4 5 6

2 minister for defence – lance corporal – private – captain
1 2 3 4
– general – sergeant
5 6

3 great grandfather – student – infant – toddler –
1 2 3 4
schoolchild – grandfather
5 6

4 oxygen – lead – wood – water – gold – steel
1 2 3 4 5 6

5 sparrow – blackbird – eagle – wren – pigeon – condor
1 2 3 4 5 6

6 Christmas – Advent – Remembrance Sunday –
1 2 3
New Year – Boxing Day – Easter
4 5 6

In problems ③-⑥ (on the following pages) the patterns of the symbols in the squares to the left of the vertical dividing line have to be discovered.

Each row has then to be completed by one of the squares to the right of the vertical dividing line, and marked by the letter (a) (b) (c) or (d).

Note in this connection that you don't (as in example 1 in problem ③ necessarily proceed from the first square to the second, from the second to the third, etc., in order to discover the pattern.

You may be able just as easily to jump from the first square to the third, and from the second square to the fourth, to find the pattern. That applies if proceeding one square at a time doesn't help. In these somewhat more puzzling cases one of the squares on the right-hand side must be the first logical step, and three squares on the left.

③

1 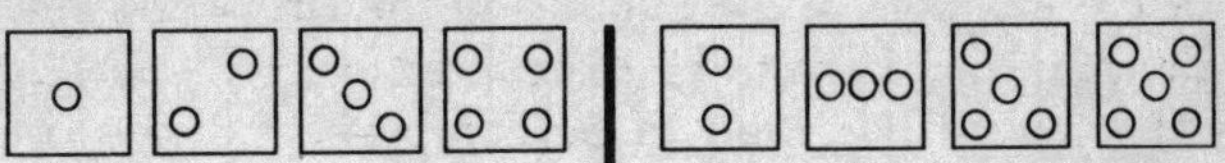

a b c d

2 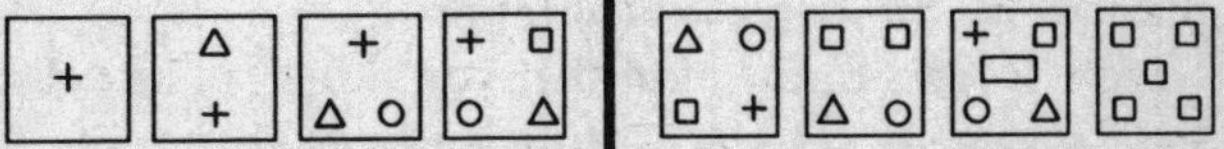

a b c d

3 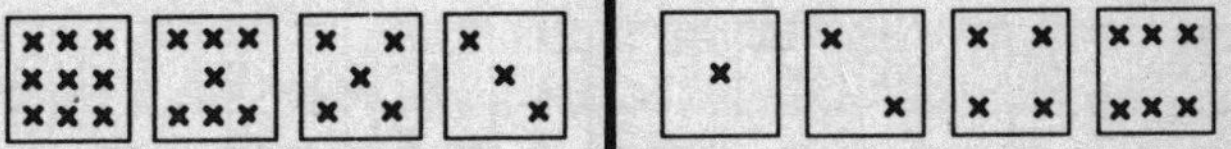

a b c d

4 

a b c d

5 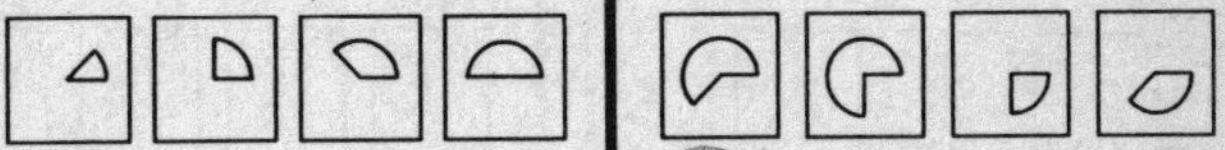

a b c d

6 

a b c d

7 

a b c d

8 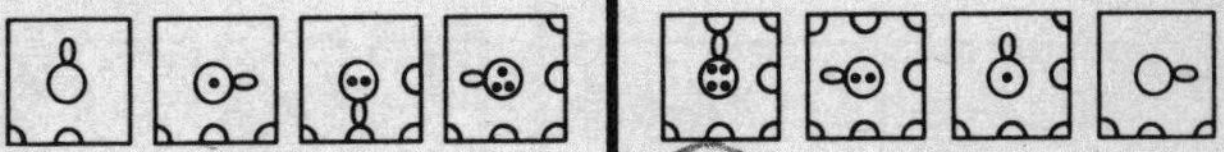

a b c d

④

1 

2 

3 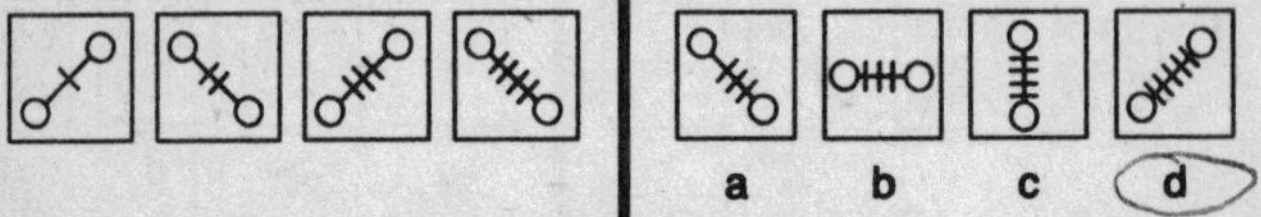

4 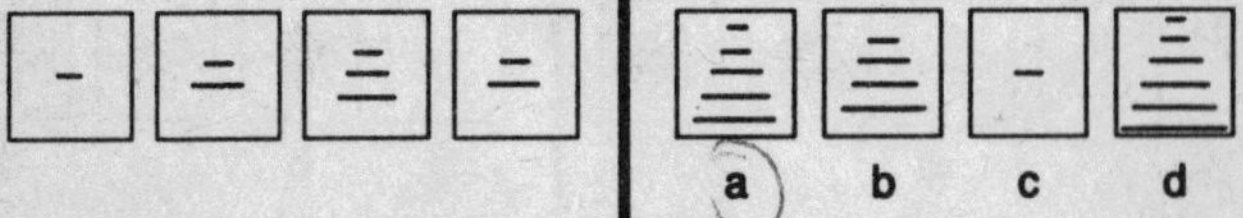

5 

6 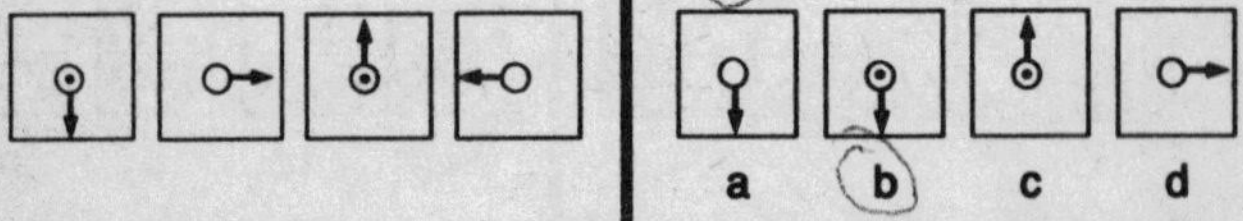

7 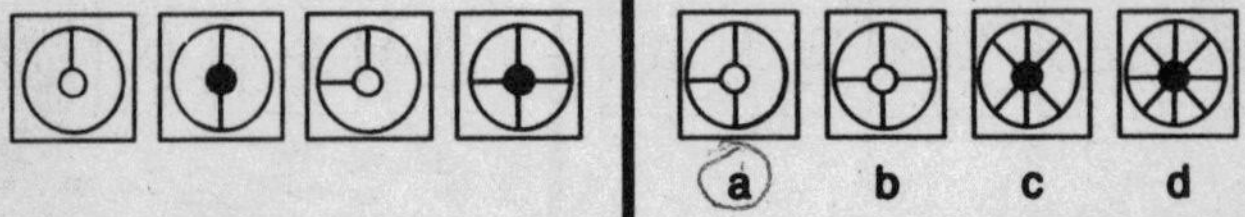

8 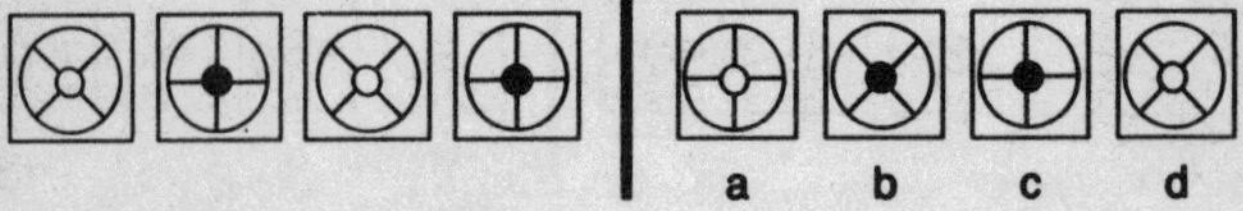

⑤

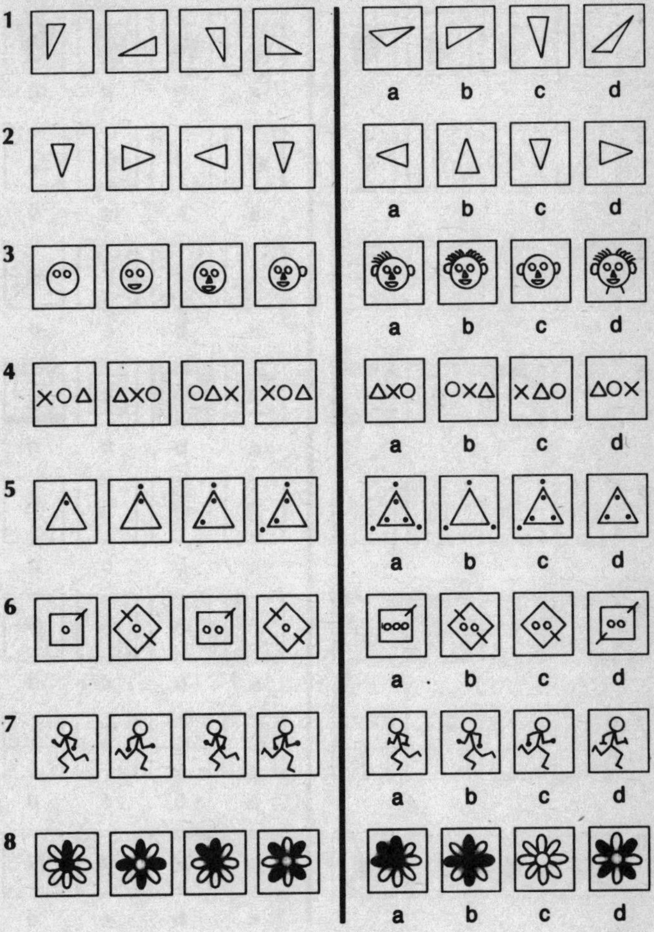

⑥

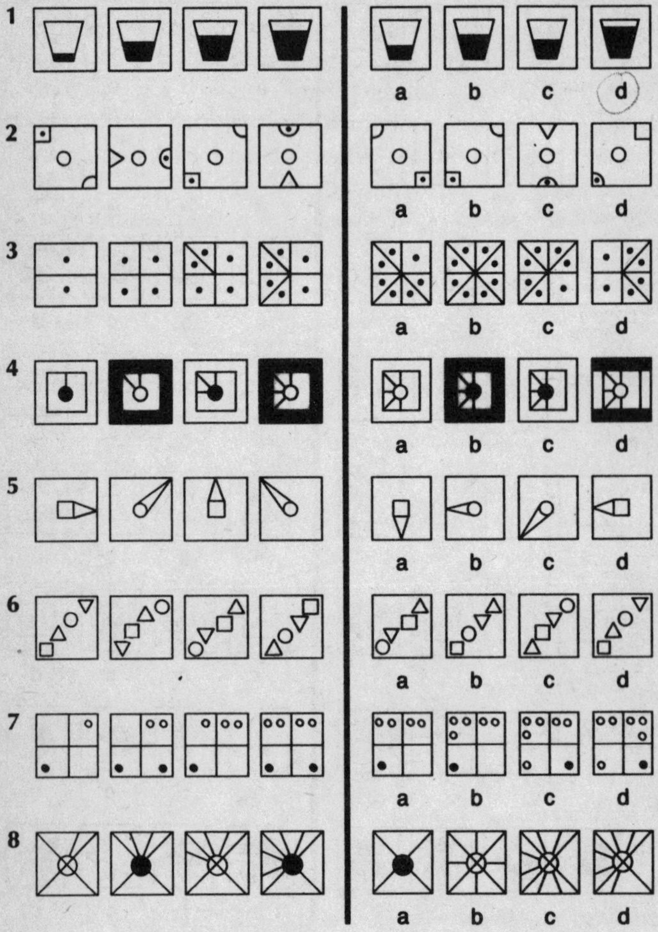

6 *Spatial concepts*

In the first exercise, groups are to be formed using only 5 figures. What you are concerned with here is the individual figure and its mirror image. You have to identify the figures that form the majority group. The majority are the figures which occur more frequently (either figure or mirror image).

To find the answer you have to turn each figure in your mind's eye so that they are all aligned on the same base.

Name the members of the majority or mark them with a cross.

Example:

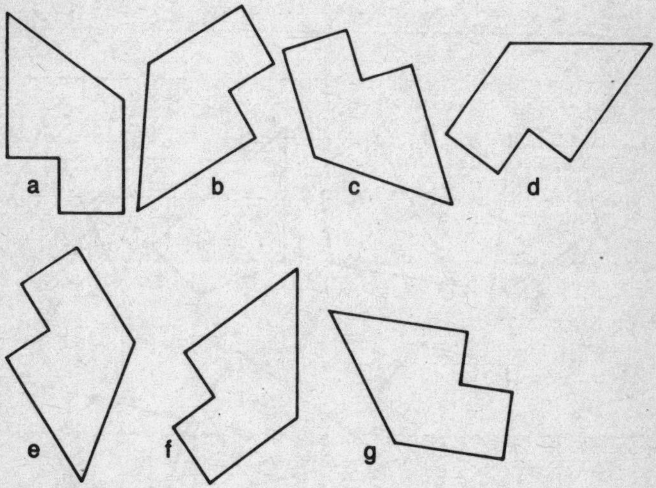

Answer: a – b – c – f

This figure occurs four times, and therefore makes up the group (majority). The mirror image appears three times as d – e – g (minority).

①

1

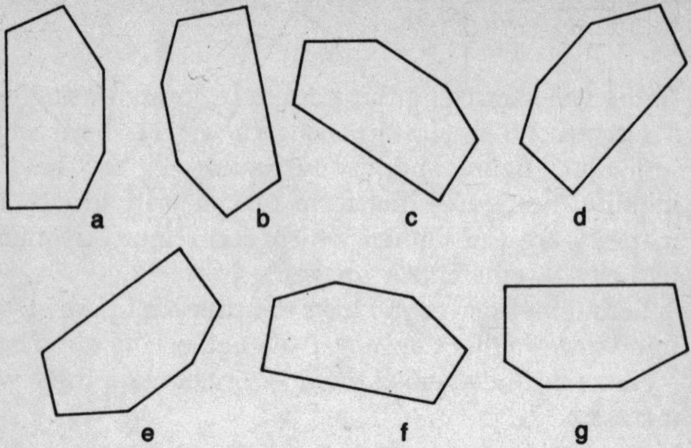

2

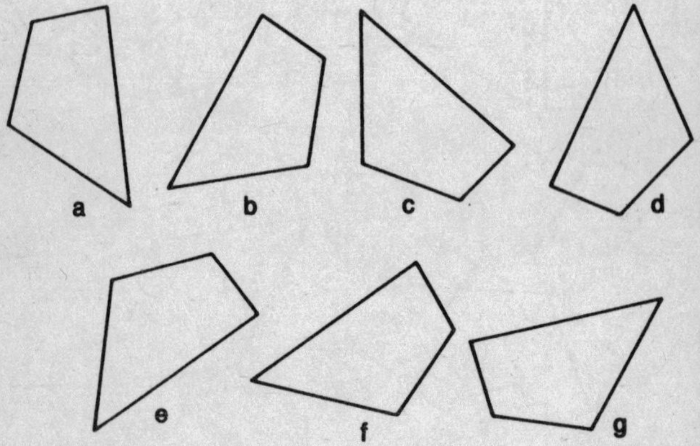

3

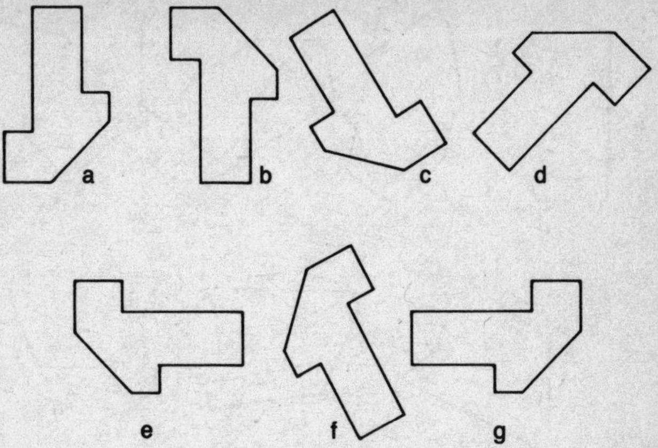

4

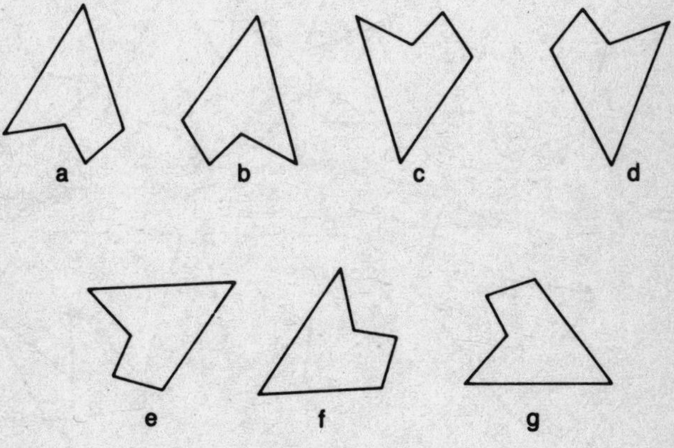

5

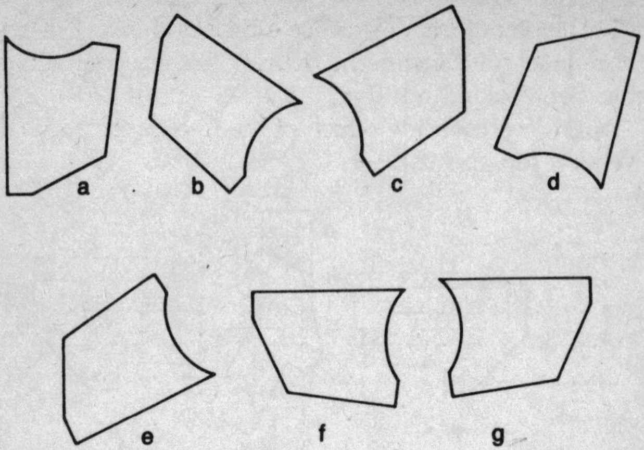

6

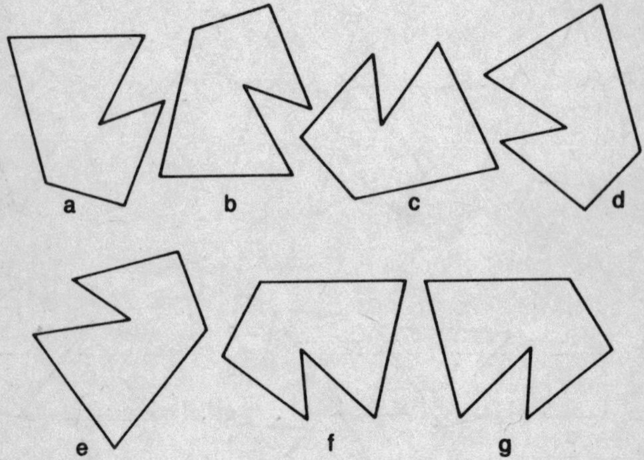

② The second set of practice exercises shows 4 sketches of regular solid geometric figures. To their right a figure has been folded out flat.

You have to decide which of the figures this unfolded version represents.

1

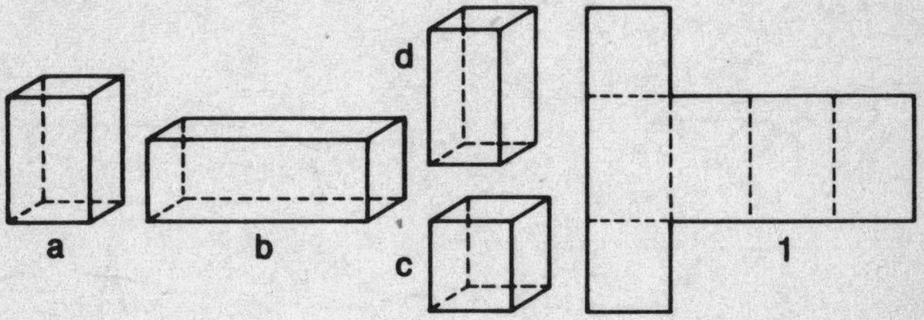

2

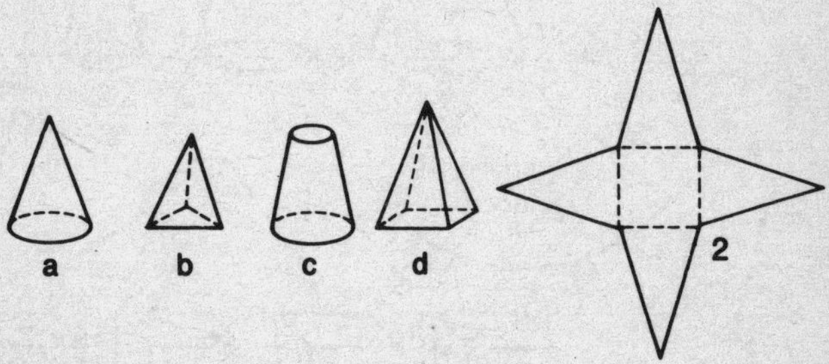

3

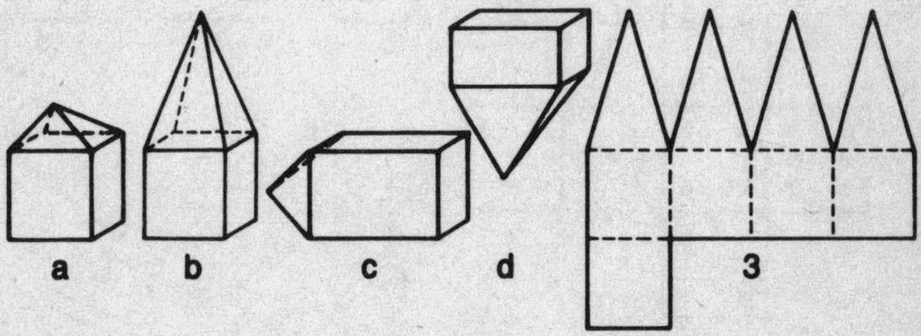

4

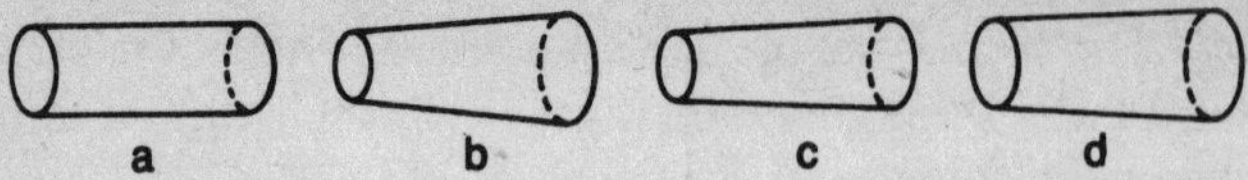

4

5

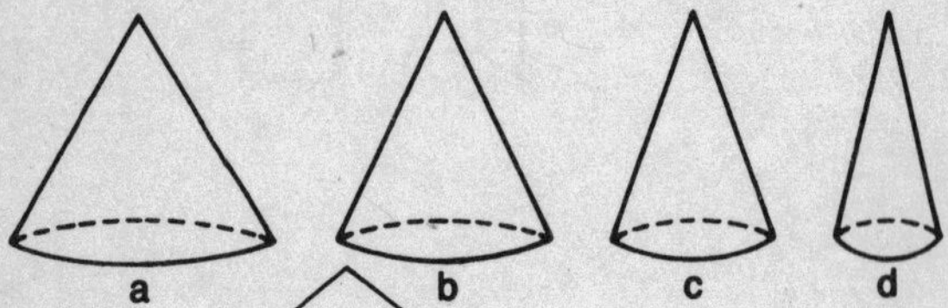

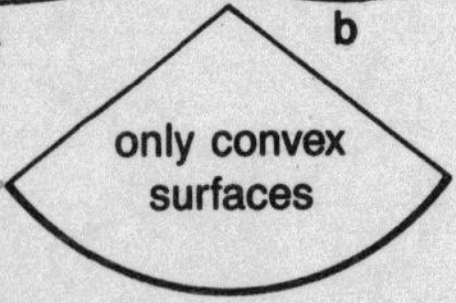

5

6

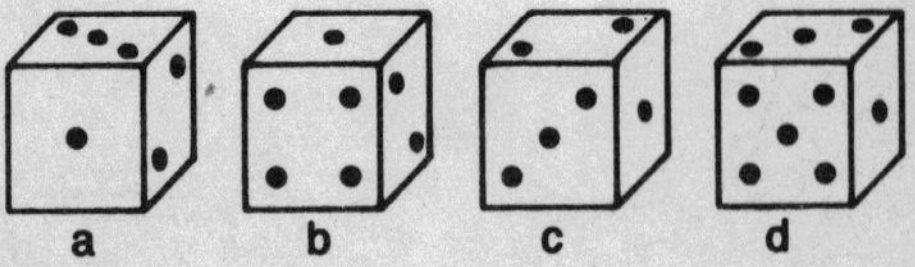

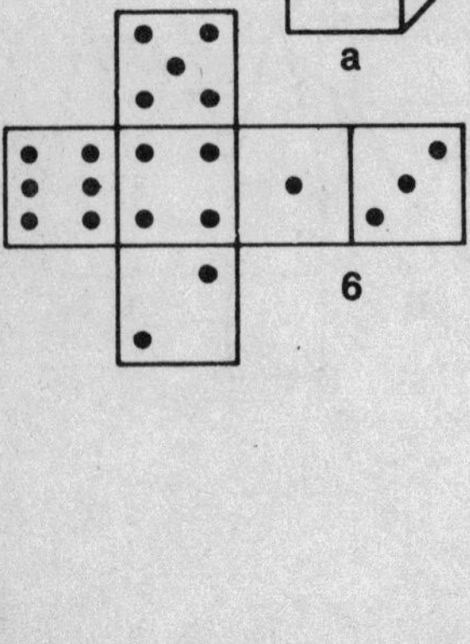

6

③ Here you are given a geometric figure which can only be made up from three out of the four segments shown.

Name or mark with a cross the three segments from which this figure is made up.

You must not, of course, trace or cut out the partial sections.

1 a b c d

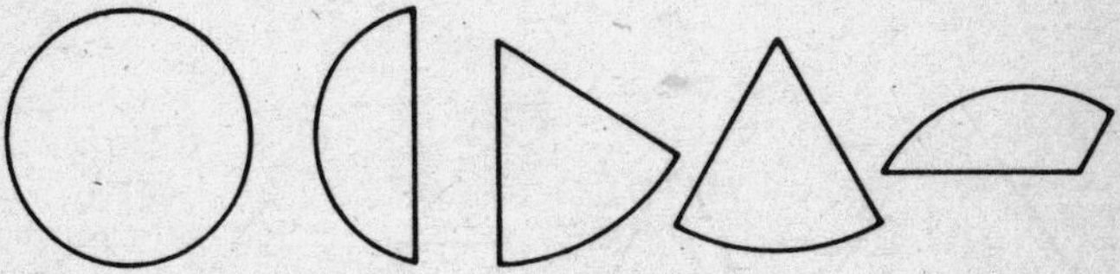

2 a b c d

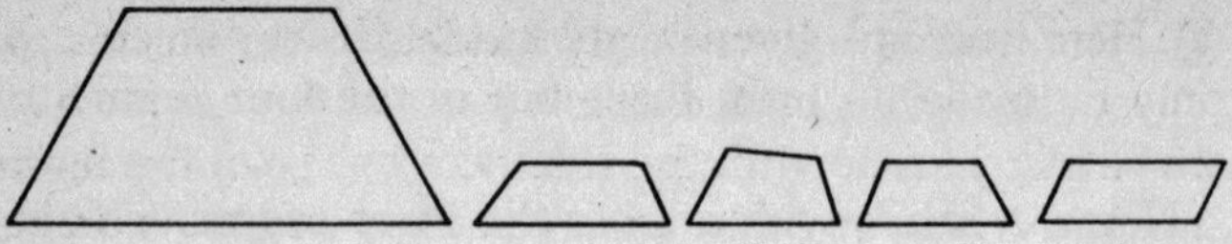

3 a b c d

4 a b c d

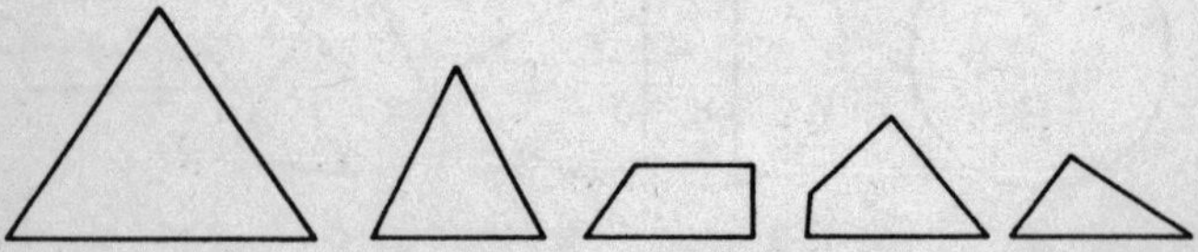

5 a b c d

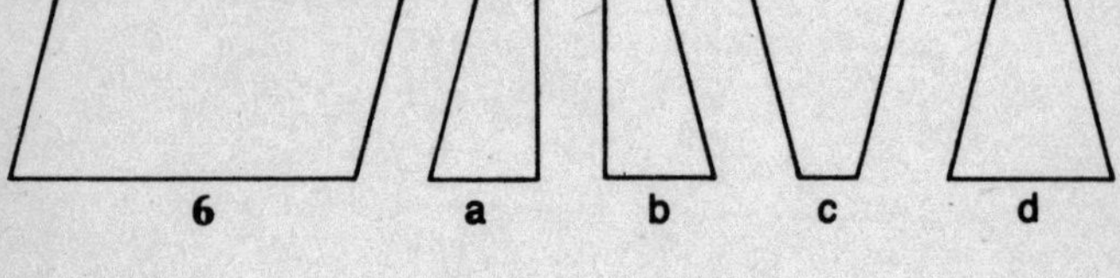

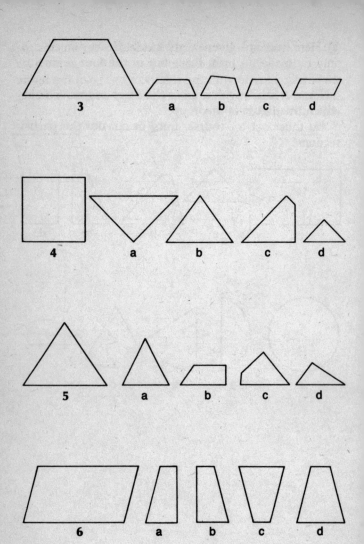

6 a b c d

④ The figures 1-4 are partly hidden under an opaque sheet. The letters on the visible parts of the figures have to be matched up with the numbers 1-4, i.e. if the figure marked A belongs to the square marked with the number 1 it must be labelled A-1.

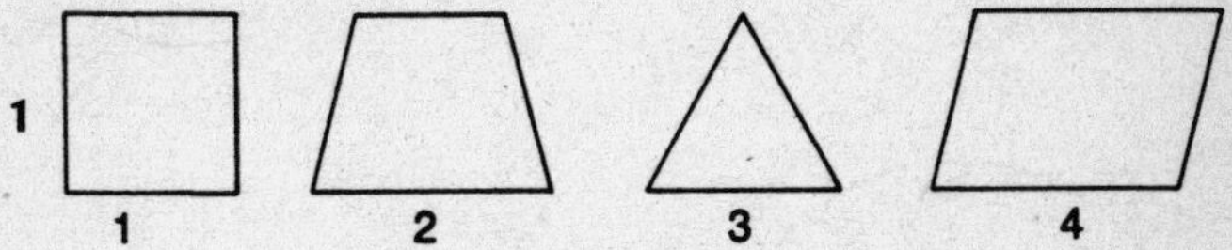

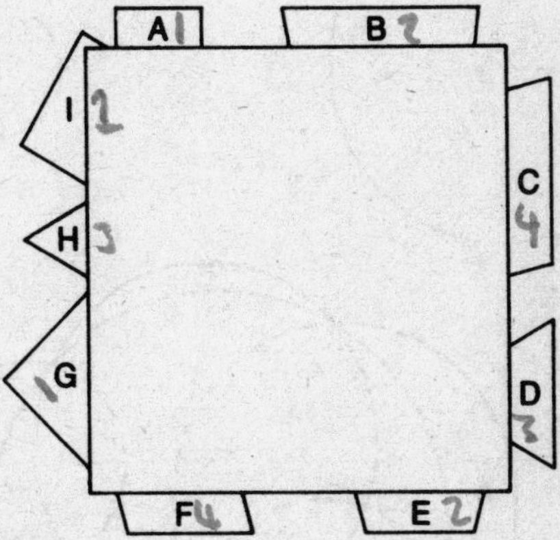

2

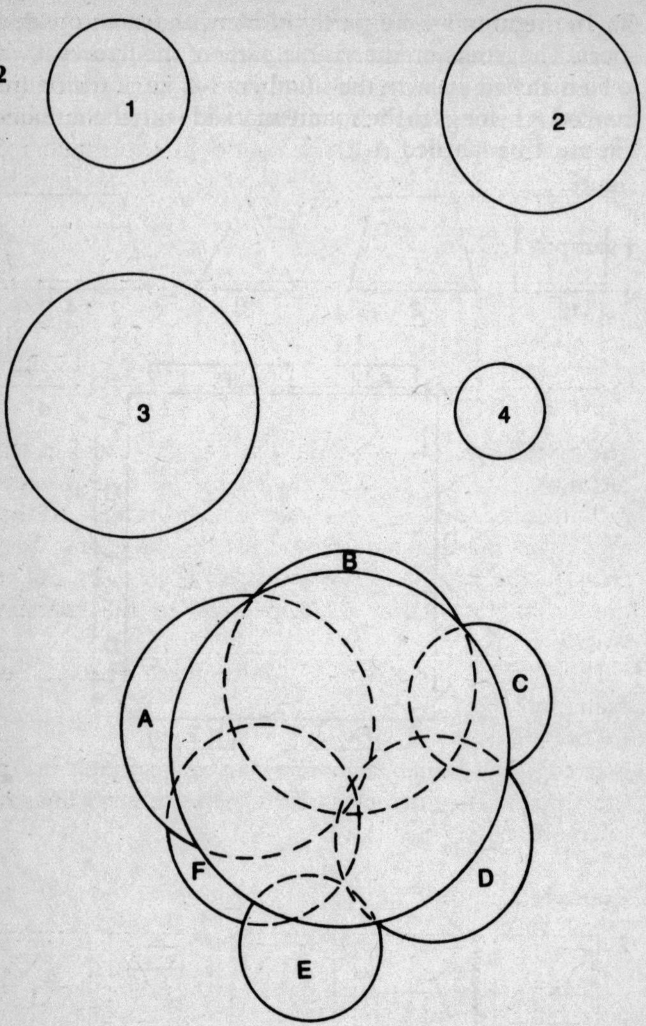

⑤ In the numbered figures only one is marked with a cross.

Find the one among the figures a to d in which the conditions are right for adding a cross in the same circumstances that are to be found in the numbered figure.

Example 1

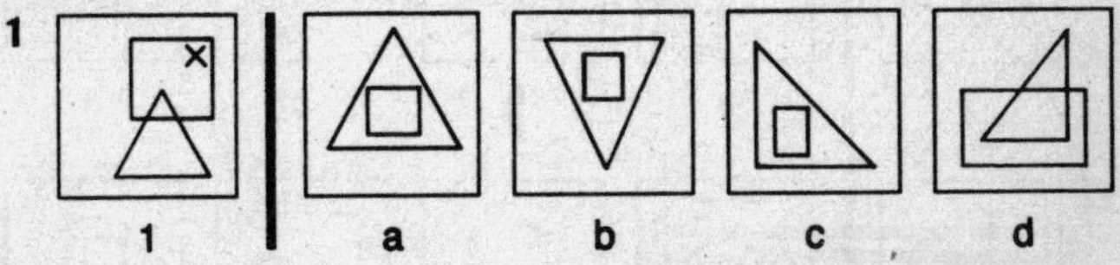

The numbered shape on the left has the cross in the rectangle, but not in the triangle. In a, b and c the rectangle is completely enclosed in the triangle, so that a cross in the rectangle would at the same time be a cross in the triangle. Only in d can a cross be put in the rectangle without its appearing in the triangle. Answer: 1d.

This can be done similarly with three shapes. See example 2.

Warning: The crosses do not have to lie absolutely inside the shapes. They can also lie on the peripheral lines or intersections of lines.

Example 2

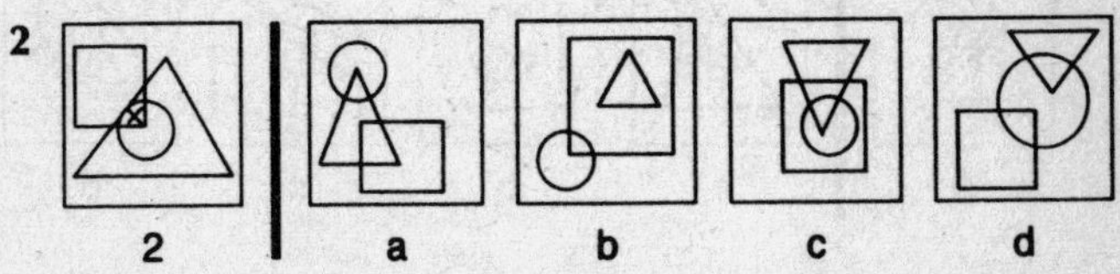

The cross in the shape on the left is in the same common section of the triangle, square and circle.

The conditions for adding a cross are only fulfilled in c, for here there is a common section (all three shapes overlap each other) in all three shapes. Answer: 2c

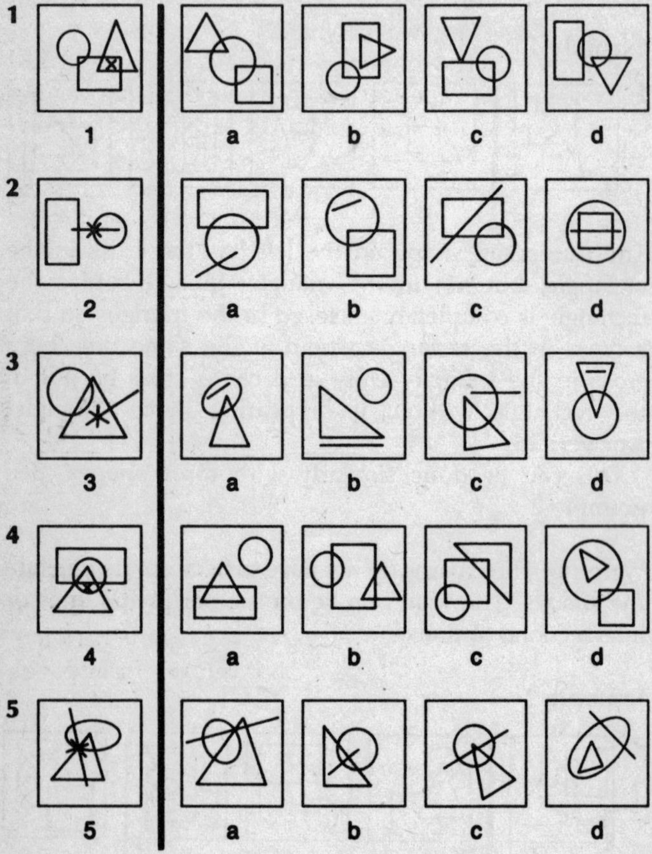

6

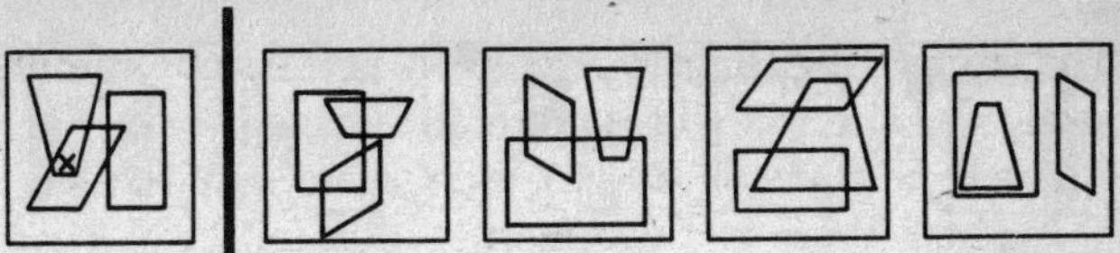

6 a b c d

⑥ The five different cubes a to e have a different symbol on each side. Only three symbols are visible.

Starting with the numbered cubes 1-8, you have to find (if possible) an identical cube (or cubes) from among those lettered a – e. Cubes 1-8 are, of course, very much mixed up.

Mentally you have to turn and twist the cubes, to decide which are the same, so that numbers and letters can be matched.

Example

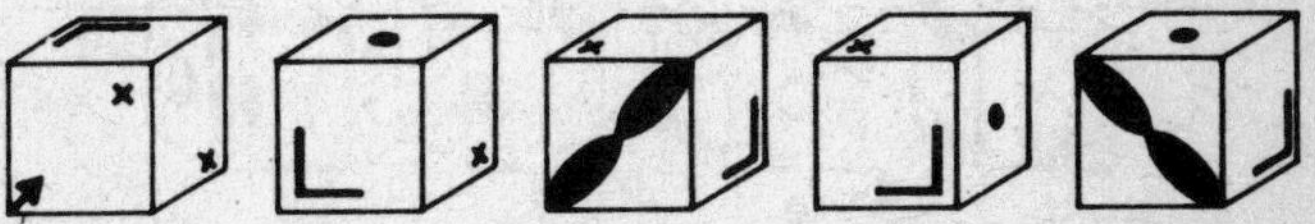

a b c d e

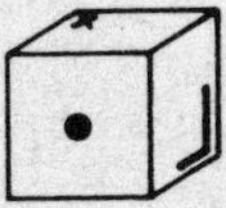

1

Answer 1b
Tip cube b to the left so that the cross comes to the top (back right). Then turn it to the left so that the cross at the top is at the back left. That way, the dot comes to the front panel.

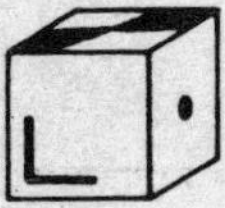

2

Answer 2e
Tip backwards, then turn to the left.

1

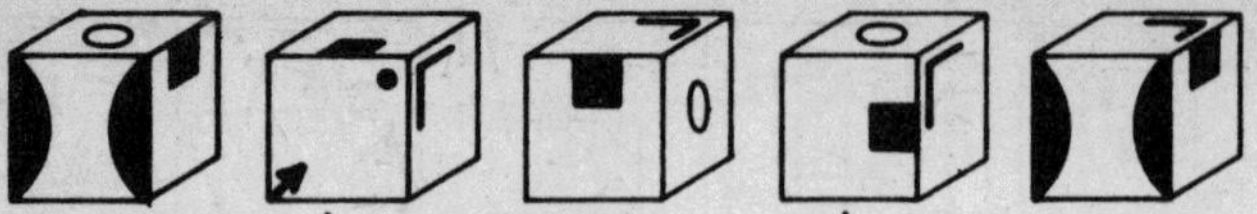

a b c d e

1 2 3 4

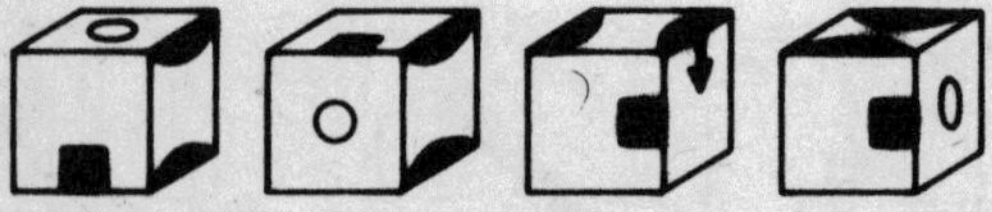

5 6 7 8

2

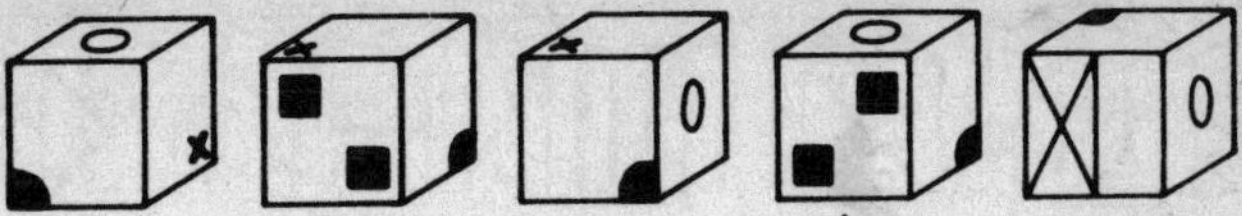

a b c d e

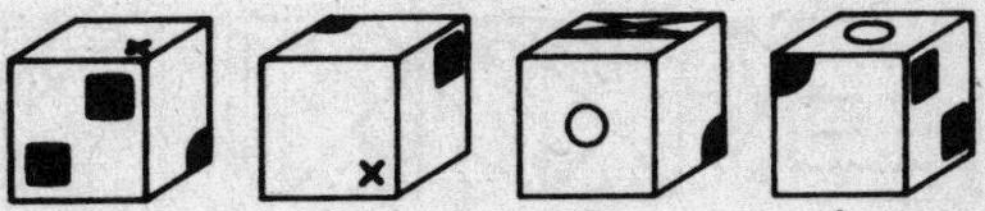

1 2 3 4

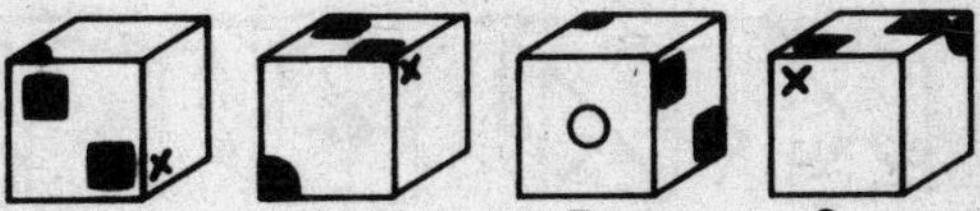

5 6 7 8

3

a b c d e

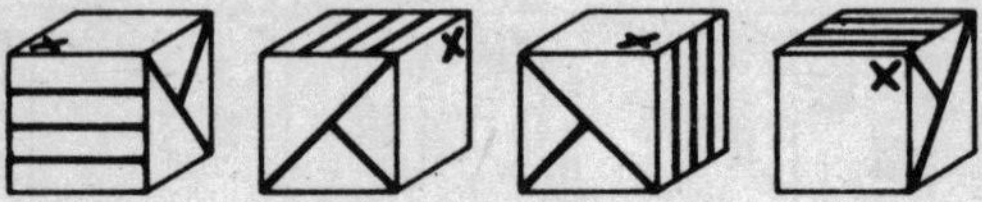

1 2 3 4

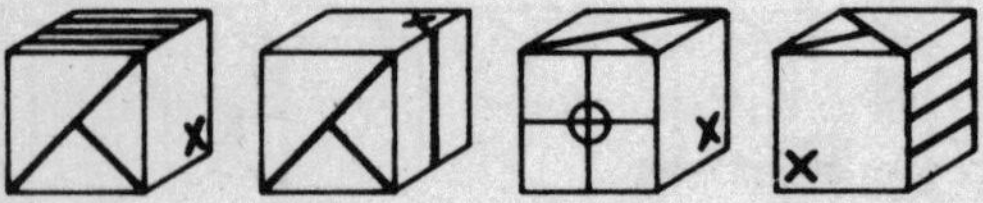

5 6 7 8

7 *Ability to observe and remember*

In this section you should concentrate on fixing lists, drawings and text carefully in your mind, as in test conditions time is limited.

What you need is intense concentration so that under pressure you can prevent any distracting details from coming between observation (impressing on the mind) and memory (responding to questions).

The questions relating to the items on observation, ①-⑥, follow at the end of this section. You will be very quickly surprised how little and how vaguely you have fixed details in your mind in spite of subjective impressions to the contrary.

Those of you who do not rate your own powers of observation too highly should read just one item at a time and tackle the relevant questions at the end of the section immediately afterwards. Those who are more confident should go to the questions after reading two or more observation exercises.

The sections 'Ruth', 'fence' and 'drawings and symbols' are relatively easy. 'Householder', 'Groups, and 'Addresses' are more difficult.

As the ability to observe and memorise is a desirable qualification for any job, you should examine yourself critically here.

① 'Ruth'

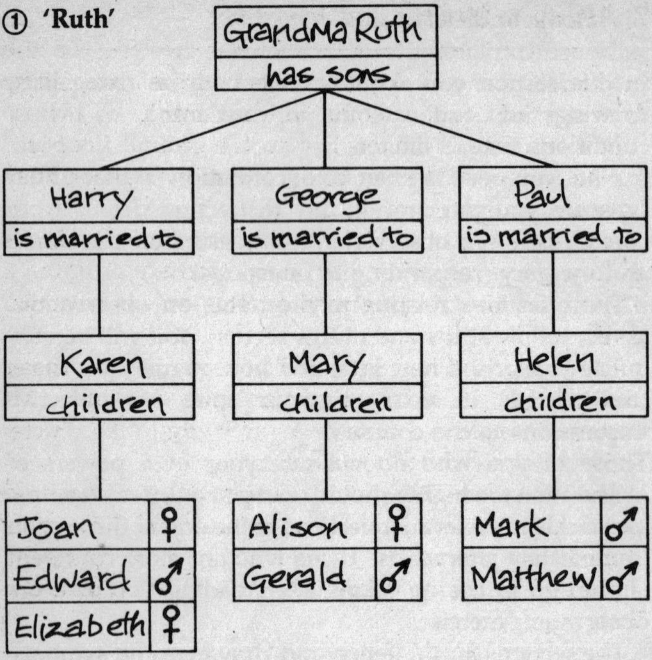

② 'Fence'

③ 'Householders'

A house containing four families has two flats on the ground floor and two upstairs. The house is occupied by four married couples (some with children).

Ivor and Edna Williams live on the ground floor left. He is a 48-year-old lawyer. She is 46 and is a teacher. They have two daughters.

Above the Williamses live the Jordans. James Jordan is a 46-year-old engineer. James is married to Rita, a 42-year-old playgroup supervisor. The Jordans have two sons.

The Fosters live next to the Williamses. Stephen Foster and his wife Sarah have a son and two daughters. Mr Foster is 58 years old, a shopkeeper by trade. Mrs Foster is 59 years old and a bookkeeper.

The other upstairs flat is occupied by 65-year-old pensioner Ian Sanderson and 58-year-old housewife Pauline Sanderson. The Sandersons have no children.

The children of the Williamses, Jordans and Fosters live with their parents.

④ **'Drawings and symbols'**

⑤ **'Groups'**

1 Countries:
Hungary – Romania – Bulgaria – Estonia

2 Jobs:
gardener – teacher – butcher – pilot

3 Plants:
thistle – carnation – marigold – fern

4 Fruit:
pineapple – clementine – plum – orange

5 Living creatures:
duck – bug – cat – dog

⑥ 'Addresses'

John Smithers	143 Thames Walk, London SW15 Tel. 081 218 5432
James Smithson	275 Thamesmead Way, London SW12 Tel. 081 726 3245
Jeremy Summers	150 Thamesside Avenue, London SW14. Tel. 081 411 2435
Joseph Sampson	326 Thames Road, London SW11 Tel. 081 730 4352

Questions to test observation and memory

1 'Ruth'

1 Names of the three married couples?
2 Names of the female grandchildren and their mothers?
3 Names of the male grandchildren and their fathers?
4 How many male and how many female family members are there altogether (including Grandma)?
5 The daughters-in-law visit Grandma with their sons. How many people come?
6 Grandma's sons go to the football stadium with their sons. How many entrance tickets have to be bought?
7 Of the grandchildren only Harry's last child goes to school. Name?
8 Edward, Mark and Matthew have started work. Which grandsons have not yet done so?
9 The last child of the eldest son and the first child of the youngest son visit the last child of the second son. Who meets whom?
10 Who are Mary's husband's nephews and nieces?

2 'Fence'

1 Does the little man part his hair on the right or the left?
2 Does he have eyebrows?
3 Can you see his thumbs?
4 Are nostrils shown?
5 How many fence-boards are there?
6 How many nail-heads are shown?
7 How many flowers are there altogether?
8 How many plants are there altogether?
9 How many petals has the flower on the far right (seen from the reader's viewpoint)?
10 How many leaves has each plant (not petals)?

3 'Householders'

1 Which women live upstairs on the left and upstairs on the right?
2 First names and surnames of the men in the job series: shopkeeper – engineer – pensioner – lawyer?
3 How many sons and how many daughters, in total, live with their parents?
4 Who is a bookkeeper? How old is she?
5 What does the 46-year-old woman do for a living?
6 What are the combined ages of Mrs Jordan and Mrs Sanderson?
7 What is the lawyer's name and how old is he?
8 The man on the ground floor right takes in a parcel for the woman on the ground floor left. She repays the delivery charges to her neighbour's wife. Which three people are involved?
9 Who is the youngest woman and who the oldest man in the house (names, ages)?
10 Which are the two married couples whose husbands' first names have the same number of letters, and so do those of their wives?

4 'Drawings and symbols'

1 a) The two small shapes complete the large one to make a rectangle.
   b) Only one small shape will do this.
   c) No small shape will do this.

2 a) This consists of a rectangle, a triangle, a trapezoid, and a parallelogram, where the rectangle and triangle partly overlap.
   b) The square and triangle partly overlap, the trapezoid and parallelogram are freestanding.
   c) There are five figures, of which one with four angles and one triangle partly overlap.

3 a) There are five branches on each side of the tree-trunk.
   b) There are six branches on each side of the tree-trunk.
   c) There are more branches on one side than the other.

4 a) The container top left has its handle on the left.
   b) The container below left has its handle on the right.
   c) The container top right has its handle on the right.

5 a) The sum of the numbers is 6902.
   b) The difference between the numbers is 4444.
   c) The 5 appears twice.

6 a) The house has two windows visible on its longer side, three in the gable end, two in the roof.
   b) There are eight windows visible in total.
   c) Smoke is coming out of the chimney.

7 a) Five is missing.
   b) The sum of the dots is 13.
   c) The dots are consecutive from 1 to 4.

8 a) The whiskers can be seen only on the right (as seen by the viewer).
   b) The front paws are shown.
   c) The right ear is bent over.

9 a) The complete rectangular figure consists of five rectangles and five squares.
b) The complete rectangular figure consists of four rectangles and six squares.
c) The complete figure is not a rectangle but a square.

10 a) The leaves on the stem are filled in in black.
b) The leaves on the stem are opposite each other (i.e. arranged in pairs).
c) The leaves on the stem are alternate (i.e. arranged alternately right and left).

11 a) There are three round shapes and four with angles.
b) Two shapes partly overlap.
c) There are four shapes with angles and two round shapes.

12 a) The overall figure is a rectangle, made up of twelve squares.
b) The overall figure is a square, made up of sixteen squares.
c) The overall figure is a square, made up of twenty-five squares.

5 'Groups'

1 The sequence of the first letters of the countries is:
a) R – B – E – H
b) H – B – E – R
c) H – R – B – E

2 One of the four countries has a different last letter from the other three countries. The last letter of this country is:
a) a
b) y
c) d

3 In one of the four jobs the letters 'e' and 'r' appear twice each. This job appears in:
a) 2nd position
b) 1st position
c) 3rd position

4 One of the four jobs listed has a different final letter from the three other jobs. This final letter is:
a) r
b) n
c) t

5 Two plants have the same final letter 'n'. The two others end in:
a) e and d
b) t and h
c) r and l

6 One of the plants grows typically in forests. It is:
a) moss
b) wood anemone
c) fern

7 One example in the group of fruit has a different final letter from the three others. This letter is:
a) e
b) y
c) m

8 One of the fruits also grows in Britain: It is:
a) apple
b) plum
c) pear

9 Two of the living creatures listed have the same final letter. The other two have the final letters:
a) k and t
b) t and b
c) t and p

10 One of the living creatures is a parasite. It is:
a) bug
b) flea
c) louse

6 Addresses

1 Mr Smithers lives in postal district
a) SW 14
b) SW 12
c) SW 15

2 John S's telephone dialling code begins:
a) 081 218
b) 081 726
c) 081 411

3 James S lives in:
a) Thamesside Avenue
b) Thames Walk
c) Thamesmead Way

4 The last group of numbers in Mr Smithson's phone number is:
a) 3245
b) 4352
c) 2435

5 The full phone number for Mr Summers, in the postal area SW 14 is:
a) 081 411 2435
b) 081 411 2534
c) 081 411 2543

6 Mr Summers' first name has the same number of letters as that of Mr:
a) Smithers
b) Sampson
c) Smithson

7 Mr Sampson's postal district is SW 11 and the last group of figures in his phone number is:
a) 2345
b) 2435
c) 4352

8 Mr Sampson in Thames Road dials (081) 218 5432 and is connected with Mr:
a) Smithers in SW 15
b) Smithson in SW 12
c) Summers in SW 14

9 The total of the last number in the second group of numbers (i.e. after 081) in the telephone numbers of all four men is:
a) 15
b) 16
c) 14

10 The total of the first number in the third (i.e. final) group of numbers in the telephone numbers of all four men is:
a) 12
b) 16
c) 14

Section Relevant to Work

(ability to concentrate, take stress, talent for organisation)

1 *Recognising symbols*

As many symbols, letters or numbers as possible out of a complicated list of them have to be identified and put in order as quickly as possible.

As the time allowed for doing this is very short, you cannot afford to waste it. You will be more successful if you proceed logically than if you think of several things at once or allow your mind to be diverted. In other words; if several symbols are involved, concentrate first on the first one and mark it and then work line by line. Do the same with the next symbol, and so on. A sheet of paper to cover up the lines you are not working on makes the task easier.

1 Identify the letters A to H with the symbols next to them. Enter the symbols quickly in the spaces to the right of the letters. It is impractical and time-wasting to fill the spaces from top to bottom and then go on to the next row. It is quicker to complete all the As with the identical symbol, then all the Bs, and so on.

When the test is evaluated (using the template) only the number of correct answers will count, not the sequence.

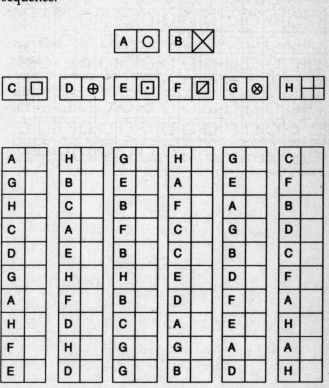

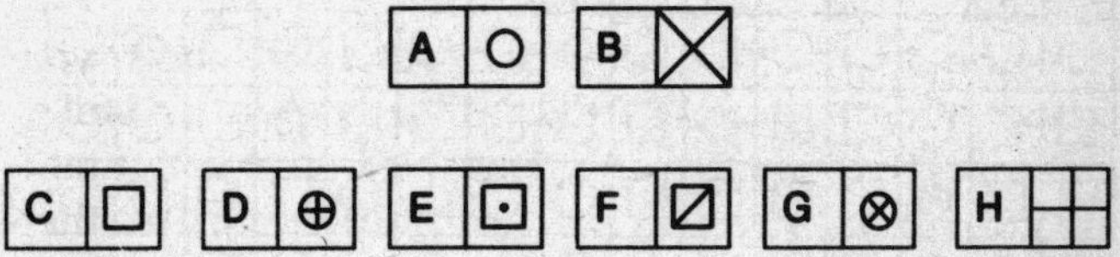

A		H		G		H		G		C	
G		B		E		A		E		F	
H		C		B		F		A		B	
C		A		F		C		G		D	
D		E		B		C		B		C	
G		H		H		E		D		F	
A		F		B		D		F		A	
H		D		C		A		E		H	
F		H		G		G		A		A	
E		D		G		B		D		H	

2 Cross out:

a) all oval shapes which have a line right and left
b) all round shapes which have a line above and left
c) all squares shapes which have a line right and below

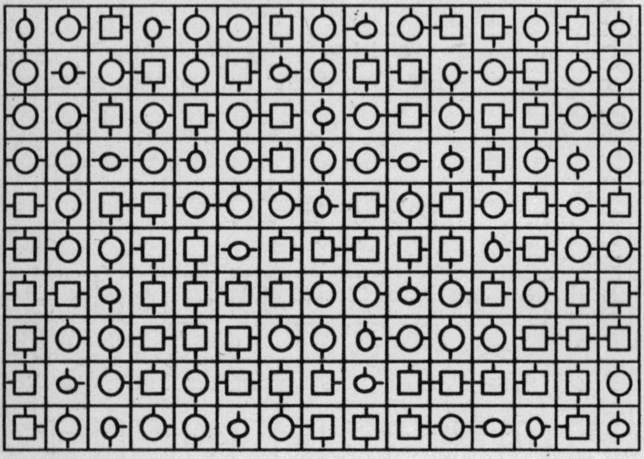

3 Put numbers in the symbols:

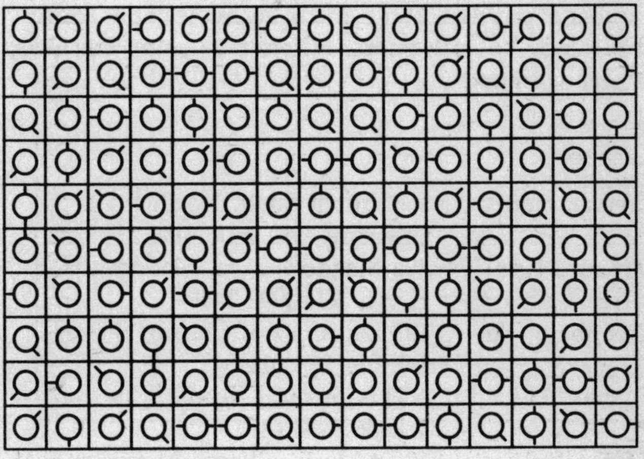

2 *Correcting mistakes in copying*

1 Compare the first list of addresses with the copy opposite. Mark the mistakes in the copy. Record the number of mistakes at the end of each line of the address in the copy. In each address there may be no mistakes, or one or more.

Addresses

Greene, Henry	16 Church Road, Northwich, Cheshire. Tel. 0606 4140
Davison, Ann	29a Meadow Lane, Hoddesdon, Herts. Tel. 0992 1440
Greenberg, Roy	102 London Rd, Cheam, Surrey Tel. 081 393 0144
Wyman, Gerald	4 The Green, Cheadle, Cheshire Tel. 061 437 4401
Calder, Paul	18 St Martin's Lane, Aberystwyth Tel. 0970 0246
Miller, Fred	5 Station Approach, Clacton, Essex
Lancaster, Jean	82 Westmorland St, Bexley, Kent Tel. 081 303 6042
Tandy, Louise	44 Smith St, Bradford-on-Avon, Wilts. Tel. 02216 5402
Wood, Dorothy	15 Mill Lane, Formby, Liverpool L37. Tel. 07048 4520
Winter, Oliver	11 City Square, Manchester M33 Tel. 061 962 2405

Copy

Green, Henry	16 Church Rd, Northwich, Cheshire. Tel. 0606 4410
Davison, Ann	29a Meadow Lane, Hoddesdon, Herts. Tel. 0992 1440

Greenburg, Ray	102 London Road, Cheam, Surrey Tel. 081 395 0744
Whyman, Gerald	4 The Green, Cheadle, Ches. Tel. 061 431 4401
Calder, Paul	18 St Martins Lane, Aberyswyth Tel. 0910 0246
Miller, Fred	5 Station Approach, Clackton, Essex. Tel. 0255 2461
Lankaster, Joan	82 Westmoreland St, Bexley, Kent Tel. 071 303 6042
Tandy, Louise	44 Smith Street, Formby, Liverpool L37. Tel. 07048 4520
Woods, Dorothy	15 Millers Lane, Bradford-on-Avon, Wilts. Tel. 02216 5402
Winter, Olive	11 City Square, Manchester M33 Tel. 061 962 2405

Total no. of mistakes _____

2 The sequence of numbers in column 1 are the models. The sequence of numbers in columns 2, 3 and 4 are the copies. Cross out the numbers in the copies that differ from those in the models.

Very little time is allowed in tests for this kind of task, so that it is essential to work efficiently. Also, the time is so tightly measured that it is not normally possible for the examinee to be completely prepared in advance.

	Model	Copy a	Copy b	Copy c
1	12051935	12051955	12051835	12051935
2	24101854	24101852	24101854	24101854
3	30092010	30002010	30092110	30082001
4	15773346	17573346	15773346	15773646
5	20114612	20118612	20114611	20114612
6	37954231	38954321	37594231	37952431
7	86686808	86868808	86686088	86686808
8	74437007	74437070	73437007	74437007
9	26996269	26696269	26966296	26996296
10	68698668	66896998	68996868	68698968

3 In this and the following exercise the business is complicated and demanding because the most varied of symbols are used.

Once again those symbols which depart from the original are to be crossed out.

	Original	Copy
1	B A 5 C 7 3 0 B	B A C 5 7 3 0 B
2	X V u v x Z R S	X V u v x Z R S
3	8 8 6 8 6 8 8 6	8 8 6 8 6 8 6 8
4	S S Ƨ Я И R Ƨ Ɛ	S S Ƨ R S И Ƨ E
5	○ □ X ⊠ ○ ○ □ ⊗	○ □ ⊠ X ○ ○ □ ⊗
6	L ⅂ ⊐ ⊓ L ⅃ Γ ⊔	L ⅂ ⊏ ⊓ L ⅃ Γ ⊔
7	C Ɔ ɑ V D C C ɑ	C Ɔ D V D Ɔ Ɔ ɑ
8	V ⊓ ⊔ Λ Λ ⊓ ⊓ ⊔	V ⊓ ⊔ V V ⊔ ⊔ ⊔
9	▯ ▯ ▭ ▭ ▯ □ ▯ □	▯ ▯ ▭ ▭ ▯ □ □ □
10	8 3 ɛ 6 ə 6 8 6	8 3 ɛ 9 6 ə 8 6
11	⌐ 5 ə ƨ Ɛ 7 3 6	⌐ ƨ 6 ƨ Ɛ 7 3 6
12	△ ⌓ ▽ ◡ □ △ ◡ ⌓	△ ⌓ ▽ ◡ □ △ ◡ ⌓
13	A A b c y A A A	A A c c y A A A
14	⊙ ○ ⊡ ○ ⊕ ⊡ ⊕ ○	⊙ ○ ⊡ ○ ○ ⊡ ⊕ ○
15	∀ ⋗ Λ ⋖ A < Λ ∀	∀ ⋗ Λ ⋖ A < A V

4

	Original	Copy
1	A i 3 6 V R 9 E	A i Ɛ 9 V R 9 e
2	O X V 8 6 s K X	O X V 6 8 s K X
3	⊓ ⊔ R S 8 T ⊥ O	⊓ ⊔ Я ƨ 8 T ⊥ O
4	S T O X □ ⊔ Λ U	S ⊥ O X ⊔ □ Λ U
5	Q ⊔ X O + X O ⊓	Q ⊔ X □ + X □ ⊓
6	ƨ S V Λ R T M N	ƨ S V Λ R T M N
7	o J └ ┐ + U O ∩	o J ┘ ┌ X U O ∩
8	A c B O a e U V	A B c O a e U V
9	W M N W N И И W	W M N N W N И W
10	6 9 0 8 3 Ɛ ɘ ə	6 9 0 3 8 Ɛ ɘ ə
11	m M n O P r S c	n M m O P c S r
12	□ △ ▽ ▽ □ ○ △ □	□ △ △ ▽ ○ ○ △ □
13	V ⊔ W M N W M M	V V M M N W M M
14	8 7 6 5 9 i e u	8 5 6 7 9 i e u
15	0 8 o 6 9 8 8 6	0 8 o 9 6 8 8 9

3 *Putting letters in order*

The letters within a group of four, five or six letters make a word if they are put in the correct order. Only nouns (including names) in the singular are used. No foreign words or abbreviations are included.

When you have put the letters in order in your mind to make an appropriate word you have to mark or cross out one letter in the indicated position in the word, or enter it in a set of boxes (see Answers).

As working to time will be necessary, and as also only the number of correct answers (not rows or columns) will count, you should initially ignore combinations of letters which you find difficult.

Where there are two identical letters in a group to choose from, either can be marked, e.g.:

R T O O   ROOT – mark either 0 as you wish.

Examples

Mark the first letter of the word:
D O R L   The L is to be marked, being the first letter of 'Lord'

Mark the middle letter:
C I R A H   The A is to be marked, being the middle letter of 'Chair'

Mark the last letter:
L A W E S E   The L is to be marked, being the last letter of 'Weasel'

1 Mark the first letter

V H E I	S D I E	S E O N	G T S A
E Y T R	G P A E	M E I T	L W L A
L A B L	H N D A	D O W R	L P A M
L D N A	K S C A	E K W E	U B E C
N H I C	E F L U	T C F A	N L I A
I E D A	H A T B	W R E C	K R F O
B Y O D	O T A C	B D A N	L A F E
A E H D	E I W R	Y C A L	R T S A
R B D I	P A E T	E C R I	D A E B
A F L O	O B O K	H M T O	D A C R

2 Mark the middle letter:

W T O L E	C C R K A	S D E R S	C U E L N
P R U G O	L R O D W	W O L E B	R U O L F
R O O F L	B L E T A	C I B K R	D S P E A
R R L U E	V T L U A	G T L H I	N A M O W
M Y N O E	T T O H O	O O N P S	C T U I N
K D R N I	P A L P E	U S O M E	R G I E T
C S P A L	C S M I U	D R G A U	T H R S I
C T H A W	F E I N K	K P A L N	N S I L A
A R T E W	T L A E P	P E H E S	O B O D L
N O I N O	K A C L H	D E L I F	A B R D E

3 Mark the last letter:

O A T O T P	G G E R A A	R T I N W E	F T S R E O
R N O C R E	K P T E C O	C Y E R H R	G E I N N E
R R R O I M	R G E N F I	H R A C N O	E T I S N C
U N O G T E	E E T T R S	G I R P S N	E O E F C F
V E E E L S	D A H R E T	Z R I A D W	R B L R E A
N U O B T T	D W O I W N	T N K G I H	P R E O C P
D B I G E R	T T K E E L	H U C C R H	C A S E R U
A A B N N A	V O H E S L	T O P A T E	M U N A T U
R M A M E H	T O C R A R	L T E N T E	R I S E L V
T L A N E P	E O U L B S	M R U S M E	O R O H B C

4 *Doing calculations competently*

Calculating figures has to be done in almost any job. Those competing for places on educational courses and for jobs are therefore expected to have mastered the basics, including multiplication tables. Additionally, knowledge of mathematical terminology and symbols (calculating signs, roots, powers, etc.) is required. The use of electronic calculators is on no account permitted when sitting the tests.

In these practice exercises we are more concerned with training for an efficient and systematic approach than with solid knowledge of how to do calculations.

1 Estimating – rough calculation

The answers should not be worked out on paper.

Examples

1 $498 + 305 + 202 =$
a) 1016 b) 1005 c) 1010 d) 999

The rough calculation $500 + 300 + 200$ gives a result of 1000, so all the proposed answers appear possible at first sight. If you add the unit numbers you get 15, so that only (b) 1005 can be the right answer (the only one with 5 units).

2 $638 \times 7 =$
a) 4460 b) 4485 c) 4488 d) 4466

The rough calculation ($600 \times 7 + 40 \times 7 = 4480$) gives a result of just under 4500, after which again none of the proposed solutions can be ruled out.

Multiplying the units ($7 \times 8 = 56$) with the final number 6 produces the only correct answer 4466.

There is more help with the following problems in the Answers section.

Estimate – calculate roughly: (divide before adding)

1 $590 \times 3 + 95 \times 6 =$
a) 2340 b) 2445 c) 2324 d) 2298

2 $120 \div 5 + 12 \div 4 + 100 =$
a) 128 b) 127 c) 80 d) 130

3 $250.25 + 349.50 + 201.05 =$
a) 801,35 b) 800,50 c) 800,80 d) 799,50

4 $112\frac{1}{2} - 85\frac{1}{4} + 305\frac{1}{2} =$
a) $332\frac{3}{4}$ b) $330\frac{1}{2}$ c) $331\frac{2}{3}$ d) $333\frac{2}{3}$

5 $55920 - 32810 + 12730 - 22220 + 1180 =$
a) 15110 b) 14950 c) 14820 d) 14800

2 Using arithmetical short-cuts – recognising bluffs

Many chain problems seem tricky at first sight. They don't have to be, though, if you use arithmetical short-cuts.

If in a long chain you have to calculate +289 and −39, combine them to make +250.

When the link is ×12 and ÷12, then this produces 1. Be careful if you are multiplying by 0, as the result is then 0.

If you have to multiply/divide *and* add/subtract, do the multiplication/division first, as follows, e.g.:

$10+3\times5-15\div3 = 10+15-5 = 20$

1 $24\div3\times2\div2\times3 =$
a) 24 b) 8 c) 48 d) 84

2 $698-168+357-357+168 =$
a) 357 b) 698 c) 168 d) 430

3 $12\times3\div6\times0\times20\div4\times5\div10 =$
a) 150 b) 0 c) 100 d) 6

4 $4+6\times2-10\div5+6 =$
a) 8 b) 7.2 c) 20.5 d) 20

5 $498\div498\times\sqrt{1}\times\frac{17}{20-3} =$
a) 1 b) 0 c) 10 d) 17

6 $298+145+2+489+11+55 =$
a) 995 b) 1000 c) 999 d) 1108

7 $125+63+450+150+37+75 =$
a) 1100 b) 1000 c) 800 d) 900

8 $225+86-175-36+200-77 =$
a) 223 b) 225 c) 240 d) 229

9 $4\times9\times7\div3\div2 =$
a) 24 b) 48 c) 42 d) 84

10 $25\times11\div5\times4\div2 =$
a) 110 b) 220 c) 440 d) 330

Example 1

$$\begin{array}{ll} 16-4 = & \\ & - \\ 16\div4 = & \\ & \underline{\underline{\quad\quad}} \end{array}$$

When the numbers in the top row are subtracted (16 – 4 = 12) the result, 12, is not to be written down. Likewise, when the bottom row is divided (16÷4 = 4) the 4 may not be written down either. The minus sign to the right between both sets of numbers means that calculation must be made: first result (12) minus second result (4). Only the final answer 8 should appear above the double line.

a)		b)		c)	
26+4 =		3×8 =		25−9 =	
	÷		−		+
16−6 =	____	24÷8 =	____	7×2 =	____

d)		e)		f)	
5×7 =		7×9 =		81÷9 =	
	+		−		×
45÷15 =	____	20−7 =	____	8÷4 =	____

g)		h)		i)	
3×4 =		32÷4 =		26−13 =	
	÷		+		−
48÷12 =	____	15+5 =	____	13−5 =	____

j)		k)		l)	
4×7 =		59−17 =		63÷9 =	
	−		÷		+
9+3 =	____	49÷7 =	____	20−7 =	____

m)		n)		o)	
88−18 =		12+48 =		12×7 =	
	÷		−		−
5×2 =	____	50÷5 =	____	6×4 =	____

(time allowed: 180 seconds)

Example 2:

	×2		÷2		−2
5		4		1	
+	☐		☐		☐
3		8		9	
+	☐		☐		☐
8		6		7	
+	☐		☐		☐
7		2		5	
+	☐		☐		☐
1		4		3	

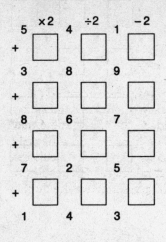

The tabulated material is longer in tests than in this example. Considerable concentration and stamina are required.

Solution to the example: In the vertical column of figures the immediate neighbours must be added up (see plus signs to the left) so that the first result noted has to be 8 (5 + 3). The 8 is then multiplied by 2, and 16 (8 × 2) must be entered in the box to the right next to the 5 and 3.

Then the vertical neighbours 3 and 8 are added, and 22 (11 × 2) put in the box.

In the second vertical row 6 is the correct number to go in the box, because 4 + 8 = 12 and 12 ÷ 2 = 6.

In the third vertical row the correct number of the first box is 8, for 1 + 9 = 10 and 10 − 2 = 8.

Answer to the example:

	×2		÷2		−2	
5		4		1		etc. →
+	16		6		8	☐
3		8		9		
+	22		7		14	☐
8		6		7		
+	30		4		10	☐
7		2		5		
+	16		3		6	☐
1	etc. ↓	4		3		

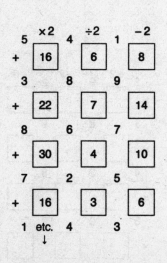

Exercise A:

		×2		÷2		−2
	5		4		1	
+		□		□		□
	3		8		9	
+		□		□		□
	8		6		7	
+		□		□		□
	7		2		5	
+		□		□		□
	1		4		3	

Exercise B:

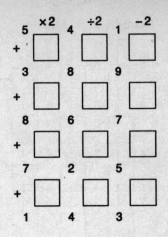

As for Exercise A, but multiply the vertically arranged numbers. From the fourth column you are required to do two calculations at the top, after the multiplication.

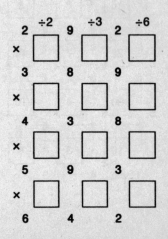

		÷2		÷3		÷6
	2		9		2	
×		□		□		□
	3		8		9	
×		□		□		□
	4		3		8	
×		□		□		□
	5		9		3	
×		□		□		□
	6		4		2	

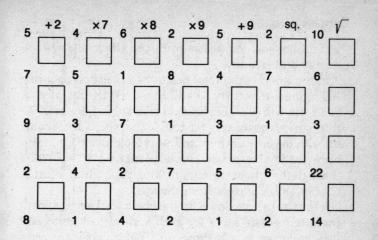

	+2		×7		×8		×9		+9		sq.		√
5		4		6		2		5		2		10	
7		5		1		8		4		7		6	
9		3		7		1		3		1		3	
2		4		2		7		5		6		22	
8		1		4		2		1		2		14	

	×2÷3		÷3×4		×5−12		÷4+12		×5+9		sq.−5		√×3
5		10		5		8		1		3		3	
3		3		4		4		3		3		3	
4		5		2		7		3		2		12	
6		6		2		4		2		5		3	
1		3		5		5		4		1		27	

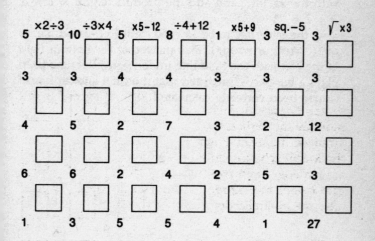

4 Being systematic

You cannot succeed unless you work efficiently, systematically and steadily.

In the exercise the total has to be calculated counting 100 figures. If you try to add these 100 figures in your head you will in all likelihood make at least one mistake through carelessness or fatigue, so that you will not come up with the answer the examiner is looking for. Once you have made this small but fatal mistake it is carried through the whole exercise, making your whole effort of concentration useless from the start.

It is safer to note down (in the blank squares provided) the intermediate totals for each vertical and horizontal line, and then to add those up. The possibility of error will be smaller and the calculation easier.

There is a further possible way to rationalise this: count the number of 1s (cross them out). Then do the same with the 2s, etc., and add the product (e.g. 6 × 1 = 6, 7 × 2 = 14 . . .)

As the table has to be worked right to the end, i.e. to the (correct or wrong) final answer, at the bottom right in the box with the bold line underneath, the time used plays a big part – provided that the final answer has of course been correctly calculated.

Example:

2	+	3	+	5	+	4	+	1	+	6	=	21
+												+
2	+	4	+	1	+	2	+	5		6	=	20
+												+
5	+	5	+	4	+	1		2		3	=	20
+												+
4	+	3	+	4		6		5		4	=	26
+												+
3	+	3		2		1		6		1	=	16
+												+
1	+	5		4		3		2		2	=	17
17	+	23	+	20	+	17	+	21	+	22	=	=
												120

If you are sure of your result, 120, it should be sufficient to add up *either* the vertical *or* the horizontal figures in the boxes. If you want to make sure of the answer you can check both ways (total vertically *and* total horizontally) and compare the two.

This procedure seems to be more efficient: count how often the individual numbers come up (cross through the numbers) then show the product.

There are:

6 × 1 =	6
7 × 2 =	14
6 × 3 =	18
7 × 4 =	28
6 × 5 =	30
4 × 6 =	24
Total	120

advantages:

- fewer calculations
- less tiring
- fewer sources of error
- quicker checking (by crossing out)

Being systematic

	1	+	2	+	6	+	3	=	
+	5		6		4		2	=	
+	7		8		7		9	=	
+	9		9		4		8	=	
+	8		1		3		9	=	
+	2		2		8		8	=	
+	9		4		6		7	=	
+	8		3		1		3	=	
+	7		4		9		5	=	
+	9		5		5		6	=	
+	7		4		4		7	=	
+	1		7		5		8	=	
+	2		9		4		2	=	
+	4		8		7		9	=	
+	9		6		9		6	=	
+	5		3		8		4	=	
+	3		2		9		8	=	
+	8		1		3		4	=	
+	7		3		6		4	=	
+	5		6		5		8	=	
+	2		4		2		2	=	
+	8		8		6		4	=	
+	4		9		8		3	=	
+	6		3		9		7	=	
+	4		9		5		5	=	
								=	

Apparently only the easiest basic arithmetical problems are set (addition, subtraction, multiplication, division). There is, however, a catch:

The working symbols (arithmetical signs) we are used to for add, subtract, multiply and divide are so fixed in our minds that we immediately and automatically add when we see a plus sign between two numbers, and we straightaway divide when we see the division sign. Here the symbols give completely different and unexpected arithmetical orders:

a plus sign now means multiply
a minus sign now means divide
a multiplication sign now means subtract
a division sign now means add

If you work along the row you must keep on checking back, to be sure which sign means what. You can easily flounder about and lose a lot of time.

It is more practical to pick out a group of problems and to solve them quickly one after another. You don't then have to reorientate yourself all the time – the associations 'plus sign means add' and 'division sign means divide' are too strongly ingrained.

So it follows simply that there are four straightforward arithmetical categories. You quickly become accustomed to the idea that in this special case the cross (or plus sign) now means 'multiply', the minus sign means 'divide', the multiplication sign means 'subtract' and the division sign means 'add'.

A comparison of both methods against the clock will prove the point.

Being practical:
Work through this page across the columns and note how long it takes in minutes and seconds.

4+8=	64−8=	72÷9=	54÷6=	48÷8=
16÷8=	7×2=	15÷5=	5×4=	8+1=
5+9=	8×4=	3+9=	7×1=	4×2=
27−9=	2+7=	5×4=	6+6=	8×7=
9×5=	15÷3=	5+7=	49−7=	20÷5=
12÷6=	18−2=	6×2=	10÷5=	8+8=
6+6=	35÷7=	36−6=	27−3=	6+6=
9−3=	8+8=	16÷2=	2+7=	8×3=
3+8=	80÷8=	5×1=	45−5=	15−5=
10×9=	25−5=	9+6=	27÷3=	8×7=
35÷5=	16÷4=	36−9=	16−4=	1+9=
5+7=	8×7=	21÷3=	9×6=	12÷3=
64÷8=	28÷4=	5+5=	9+3=	7×4=
72÷9=	10+9=	36÷4=	9×8=	21÷7=
5+5=	6×3=	10×3=	30÷5=	81−9=

Being practical:
On this page work practically and efficiently. Note the time taken in minutes and seconds and compare with the time taken to do the previous exercise.

4+8=	64−8=	72÷9=	54÷6=	48÷8=
16÷8=	7×2=	15÷5=	5×4=	8+1=
5+9=	8×4=	3+9=	7×1=	4×2=
27−9=	2+7=	5×4=	6+6=	8×7=
9×5=	15÷3=	5+7=	49−7=	20÷5=
12÷6=	18−2=	6×2=	10÷5=	8+8=
6+6=	35÷7=	36−6=	27−3=	6+6=
9−3=	8+8=	16÷2=	2+7=	8×3=
3+8=	80÷8=	5×1=	45−5=	15−5=
10×9=	25−5=	9+6=	27÷3=	8×7=
35÷5=	16÷4=	36−9=	16−4=	1+9=
5+7=	8×7=	21÷3=	9×6=	12÷3=
64÷8=	28÷4=	5+5=	9+3=	7×4=
72÷9=	10+9=	36÷4=	9×8=	21÷7=
5+5=	6×3=	10×3=	30÷5=	81−9=

Finding solutions and solving problems

Of course it is important for the trainer and employer to know if the candidate can quickly and correctly unravel and solve problems which are presented in a complicated way.

The purely arithmetical requirement is mostly small, once you have spotted the way the question works.

1 Mental arithmetic:
$835 \times 5 \div 25 \times 10 \times 0 \times 20 =$

2 The journey to work by car is 12 km.
How many km does the employee travel in a week on account of his work, for a 5-day week, making no other journeys?

3 A farmer had 17 sheep. All but nine died. How many sheep remain?

4 On average, how many birthdays does every normal healthy European man have?

5 We know that the number of days in a month is variable. So March has 31 days but April only 30. How many months have 28 days?

6 Railway track is made up of pieces of rail. Each piece should be 25m long. A single stretch of railway line (without return traffic) 300m long has to be replaced. How many pieces will be needed?

7 Divide 60 by ½ and then add 20 to it. Answer?

8 The father is 50 years old. The son is three years short of half his father's age. The son's girlfriend is 2 years younger than the father's son. The girlfriend's mother is 5 years older than double the age of her daughter. The husband of the mother of the son's girlfriend is 2 years older than the first-mentioned father. How old is the girlfriend's father?

9 The water surface of a pond is $2048m^2$. A quick-growing water-lily is planted, so that the area covered by the leaves doubles daily. The water surface is completely covered by water-lily leaves after 48 days. After how many days is the water surface

a) three-quarters covered

b) half covered?

10 A customer has to pay £7.50 and gives the cashier a £20 note. The cashier looks in the till helplessly and asks the customer if he has a £50 note. Why?

The greater the number of candidates, the broader will be the degree of competence expected and required by the company doing the selecting and employing.

At the same time, qualities will also be expected which often appear not to go together: a brilliantly creative approach on the one hand and fussy carefulness on the other.

The examiner will establish by direct comparison of the candidates' results, whose accuracy stands up more or less well in the face of the pressure of time, stress and exam nerves.

The human abilities to be tested in exercises 1 and 2 below can also be described as 'resistance to boredom'.

Exercise 1:
Only the centre of the clock faces is marked. You have to mark with a dot or a small dash on the circumference the position of the point of the minute hand of the clock for the time given.

The answers will be checked by using a template.

Example 1:

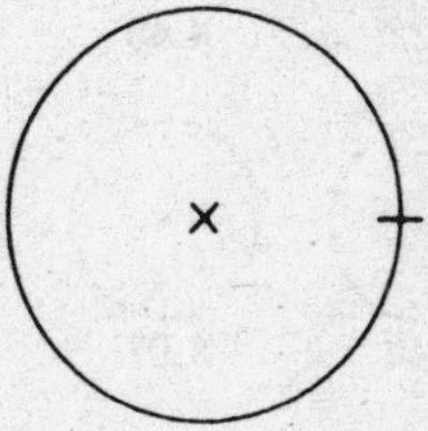

× hours 15 = × 15 (quarter past)

1

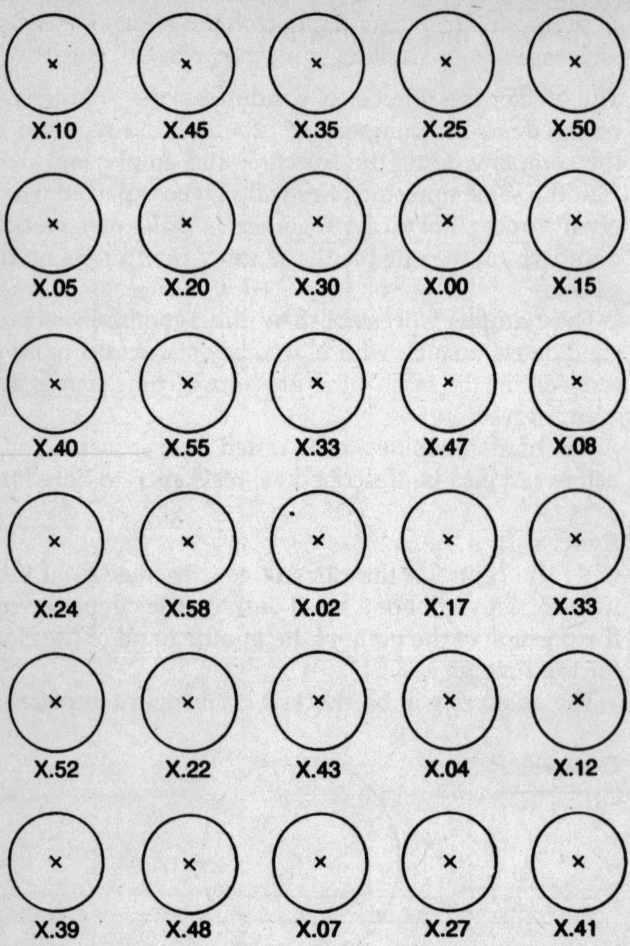
X.10
X.45
X.35
X.25
X.50
X.05
X.20
X.30
X.00
X.15
X.40
X.55
X.33
X.47
X.08
X.24
X.58
X.02
X.17
X.33
X.52
X.22
X.43
X.04
X.12
X.39
X.48
X.07
X.27
X.41

2 In the squares, draw circles by hand which increase or decrease in size. Rubbing out is not allowed. Check with the model.

3 Now we come to careful, and therefore precise, calculation and logical procedures.

Circles, squares and crosses are to be drawn neatly.

Task

1 Circle every seventh 7.
2 Put a square round every eighth 8.
3 Cross through every ninth 9 with a neat cross, the arms of which are at right angles to each other.

Count the numbers for each task from left to right.

Example

0	7	6	3		8	5	1
2	4	3	0	2	5	6	1

Warning: If you miscount, the next circle, square or cross will automatically be wrong and won't count in your marks.

1	8	4	6	0	7	7	8	3	3	0	0	7	1	1	2
2	1	4	1	8	2	0	7	3	8	3	0	2	8	4	4
3	0	6	0	8	2	0	8	1	3	0	8	0	0	3	0
4	4	0	9	2	3	8	0	7	0	7	6	2	4	1	7
5	1	2	2	7	0	8	0	9	0	6	9	2	2	6	0
6	4	3	6	0	4	8	0	1	8	0	8	6	0	4	0
7	1	6	2	3	1	4	8	9	2	1	7	9	1	0	9
8	0	4	6	7	3	0	6	9	7	8	8	9	9	1	4
9	9	4	6	9	8	8	0	2	6	6	1	9	9	3	3
10	1	3	8	0	4	1	2	9	8	7	3	0	8	0	1
11	8	5	0	9	7	3	6	0	9	3	1	1	9	8	8
12	9	9	9	1	7	8	8	5	7	2	6	7	9	9	0
13	2	3	0	4	7	8	9	4	9	0	8	0	9	1	8
14	8	0	4	3	7	7	0	7	0	3	1	6	9	7	9
15	9	1	7	9	6	6	9	0	3	9	9	9	9	1	9
16	8	4	2	7	8	0	8	9	3	6	1	9	8	9	8
17	0	4	6	9	7	7	7	9	2	6	0	3	9	0	2
18	8	8	8	0	1	9	1	3	7	7	0	7	7	1	0
19	4	0	2	6	3	0	0	8	8	7	6	9	8	7	9

6 *Organisation*

1 The examinee, as the official in charge (for a wholesale firm) must work out and list in tabular form the annual turnover rebate (discount) for 20 customers.

The following table shows the customers with their annual turnover rounded up or down, and the discount, which has been worked out for each individual according to percentage turnover.

1 Task: List customers alphabetically.

2 Task: List customers according to the turnover achieved – beginning with the highest turnover.

3 Task: List the customers according to the refunded discount – beginning with the highest £-discount.

4 Task: What was the total turnover achieved by the 20 customers?

5 Task: How much money (£) in total must be distributed to the customers in discounts?

As additional calculations will be required, please keep the facing page ready.

1	Customer	Turnover in £	Discount in %
	Maddox	25 000. –	3.0
	Madewell	100 000. –	0.3
	Madden	35 000. –	1.2
	Madeley	50 000. –	1.0
	Maddy	20 000. –	3.5
	Madison	70 000. –	0.8
	Madgett	60 000. –	0.6
	Magnet	250 000. –	0.1
	Madhani	300 000. –	0.08
	Madgwick	80 000. –	0.5
	Magee	500 000. –	0.02
	Maggs	85 000. –	0.9
	Madle	150 000. –	0.3
	Madrugo	30 000. –	1.6
	Madistone	90 000. –	0.6
	Magilner	125 000. –	0.3
	Magley	45 000. –	1.5
	Magilton	95 000. –	0.5
	Magness	75 000. –	0.8
	Magill	15 000. –	3.5

1st Task Alphabet	2nd Task Turnover in order		3rd Task Discount in order	
Name	Name	Turnover	Name	Discount
	4th Task		5th Task	

2 A security company arranges for the surveillance of a property, round the clock, seven days a week, using only part-time staff. The employees can be used at the most in two shifts of eight hours each.

There are 10 part-time staff to look after this property. Some of them can be used only on early shifts (E), only on late shifts (L), only on night shifts (N), on early and late shifts (EL) or on all shifts (A).

In addition, outside help can be called on for a maximum of two shifts each week for all shifts (OH).

Nine of the ten part-time staff (excluding Arnold) have expressed the wish to have their shifts on consecutive days. Moreover Derek and Maurice are not able to change shift during the week, i.e. if on their first day's duty they are on early shift, the next day has to be an early shift again. The same goes for the late shift.

Arnold, who is available for any shift, wants particularly to work only nights or Sundays, because those are paid better.

Double shifts or two shifts in one day are not possible.

Part-time staff:		Outside help:
Arnold (A)	Sam (N)	Charlie (OH)
Derek (EL)	John (E)	
Frank (A)	Ken (N)	
Harry (L)	Maurice (EL)	
Henry (E)	Albert (L)	

2 Possible weekly timetables

Shift	Mon.	Tue.	Wed.	Thur.	Fri.	Sat.	Sun.
Early							
Late							
Night							

Shift	Mon.	Tue.	Wed.	Thur.	Fri.	Sat.	Sun.
Early							
Late							
Night							

Shift	Mon.	Tue.	Wed.	Thur.	Fri.	Sat.	Sun.
Early							
Late							
Night							

What is needed here is a basic knowledge of physics and an appreciation of the laws of physics (e.g. leverage, mechanics, rotary movement). Formal learning is not a prerequisite. Thinking about how physics works is more important than profound knowledge.

As the problems mostly refer back to a few basic principles, training with the following exercises should be sufficient. If, however, you want to pursue a career which requires advanced technical knowledge, you would do better to take your physics textbook and work through the chapters relevant to your needs.

1

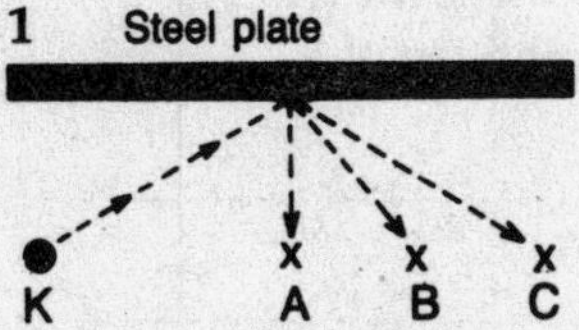

In which direction will the steel ball K rebound from the plate?

A B C

2

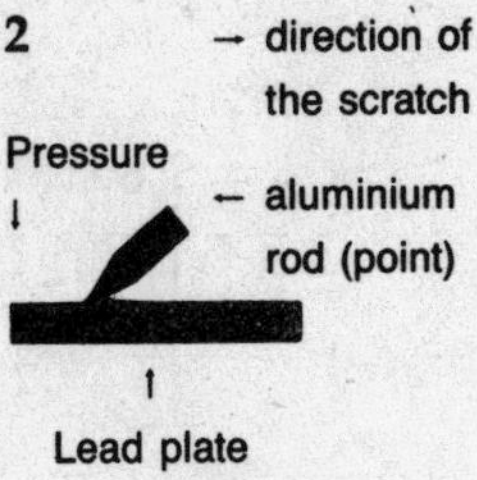

A pointed aluminium rod is drawn from left to right across a smooth flat lead plate.

Result:

A The point of the aluminium rod is badly crumpled
B An indentation is made on the lead plate
C No impression of a scratch is apparent.

3

Steel hammers with wooden handles:
With which hammer will the biggest blow be struck?

A B C

4

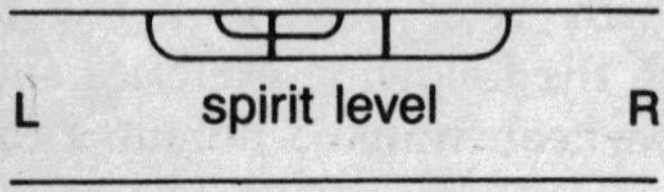

When is the spirit level balanced?

A The level is in balance
B The level has to be lifted to the right (R)
C The level has to be lifted to the left (L)

5

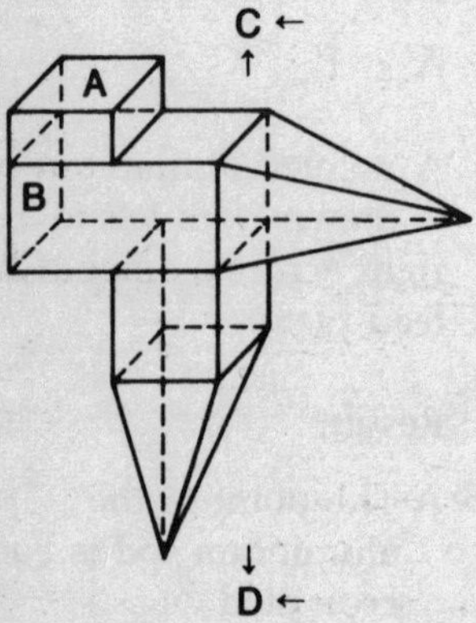

A If the figure is placed on surface A it will remain upright.
B If the figure is placed on surface B it will tip over towards D.
C If the figure is placed on surface B it will tip towards C.

6

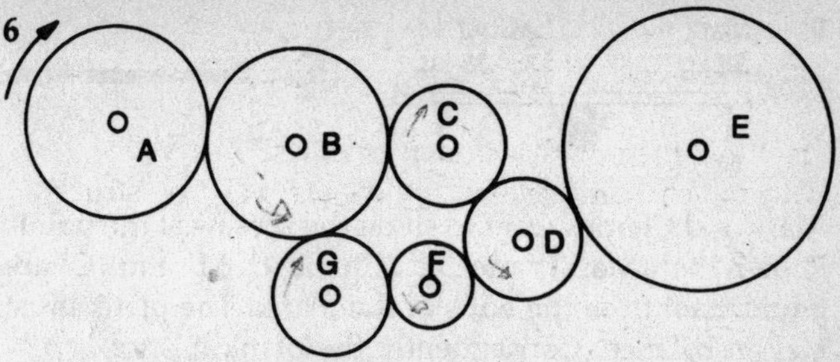

Cogwheels: the driving wheel should turn to the right.

A Cogwheel F will turn the fastest
B Cogwheel E will turn to the left
C The system doesn't actually work

7 The diesel engine of a private car with 6 cylinders, 1875 ccm cylinder capacity and 90 horsepower output, has

A 6 sparking plugs
B 12 sparking plugs
C no sparking plugs

8

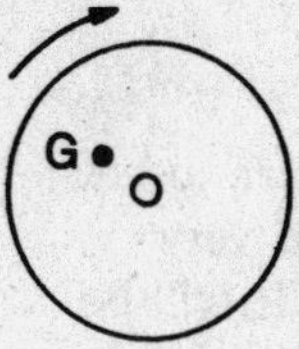

An object, G, is placed on a horizontal disc. The disc is set in motion in the direction of the arrow and goes faster and faster.

A G holds its position
B G slides to the centre
C G slides away towards the edge, in the direction in which the disc is turning.

9

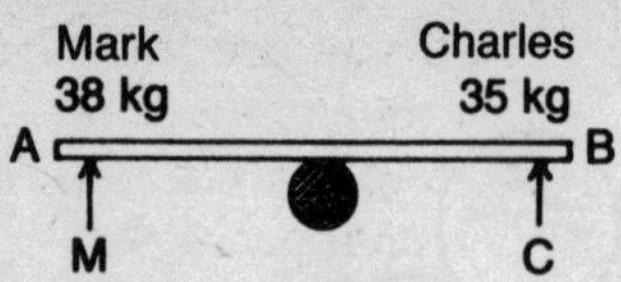

Mark and Charles want to sit on the seesaw at the points shown M (Mark) and C (Charles). M and C are equidistant from the ends of the plank. The plank must stay in balance. Consequently the plank has to:

A be moved in direction A
B be moved in direction B
C be left as it is

10 Screwdrivers

A very firmly embedded screw has to be loosened with a screwdriver, without other mechanical or chemical help. This will be done best with

A B C

11

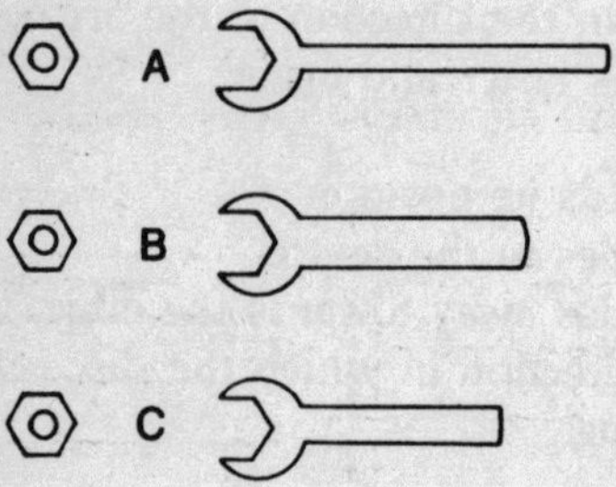

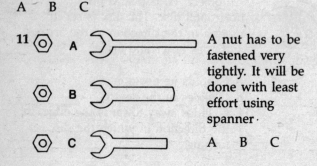

A nut has to be fastened very tightly. It will be done with least effort using spanner

A B C

12 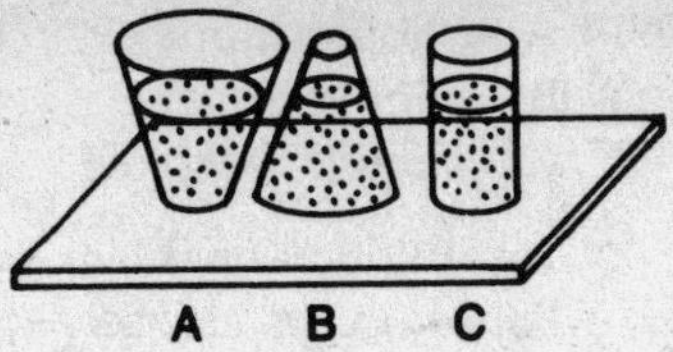

If you use the same amount of force, which container is the hardest to tip over:

A B C

13 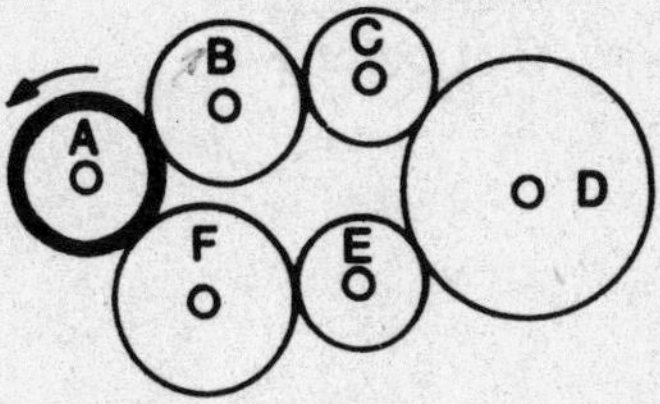

Cogwheels: Wheel A is the driving wheel of the system.

A Wheel D turns the same way as wheel A

B The system doesn't work

C Wheel E turns the same way as wheel A

14 A wooden frame is to be supported effectively in such a way that the stability of the structure takes priority, but at the same time the use of materials is to be economical. The supports are excellent. The most effective solution is:

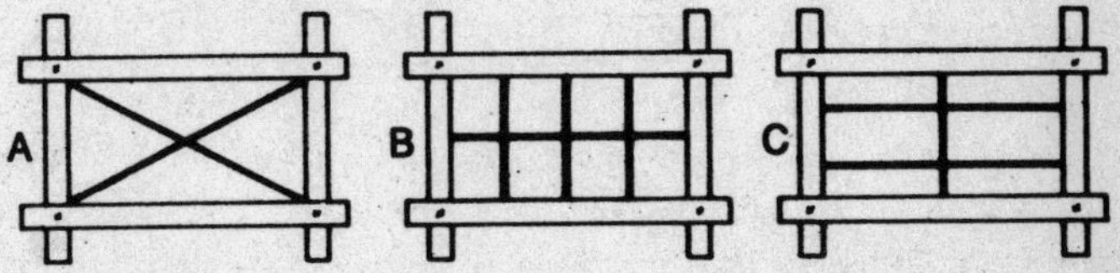

15

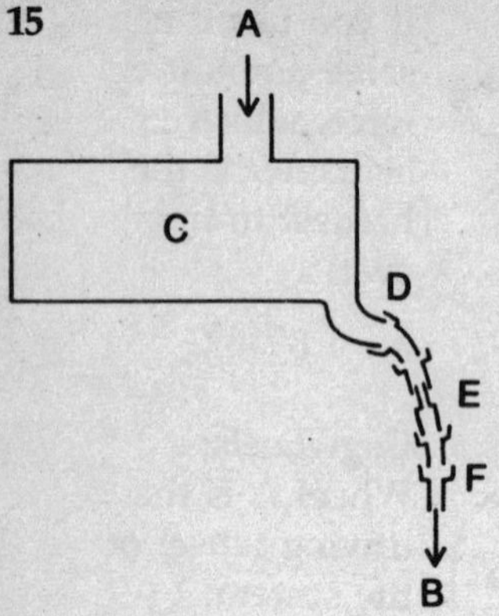

A = liquid input
B = liquid outlet
C = liquid reservoir

An unintentional leak of liquid occurs at one point.

A at point D
B at point E
C at point F

General knowledge and school subjects

General knowledge questions are often put together randomly and arbitrarily, so that focused training is problematical. If the examinee has absorbed little outside the home, it is difficult to prepare him or her in any way.

Preparation is made more difficult in that there is a vast range and quantity of subject areas which the examiner can count as general knowledge and from which he or she can choose.

Often, too, examiners ask for facts or about subjects in which they are by chance themselves especially knowledgeable or with which they have a particular connection.

As a small sample, here are a few questions covering the following areas:

- general knowledge
- history/politics
- geography
- biology
- physics/technology

1 *General knowledge*

1 How many angles has a traffic stop sign (not the manually operated road works stop sign)?
2 What is the plural of 'criterion'?
3 How many legs must a table have if it is not to be unsteady?
4 Why are there *five* Olympic rings?
5 What is the origin of the military custom of saluting (hand to cap)?
6 Why is the handbrake in cars for British roads always to the left of the driver?
7 How do the holes get into Swiss cheese?
8 'A and O' mean 'beginning and end'. Why?
9 How does a tall-masted ship get into a bottle?
10 What does the raised sign ® mean after the names of many products?

2 *History/politics*

1 What countries make up (a) Great Britain, and (b) the United Kingdom?
2 Which monarch preceded (a) Queen Elizabeth I and (b) Queen Elizabeth II?
3 For what purpose, and approximately when, were the pyramids built in Egypt?
4 What does the inscription INRI on the Cross mean?
5 What crosses are represented on the Union Jack?
6 What year was (a) the battle of Hastings and (b) the battle of Trafalgar?
7 In which year did the Russian Revolution take place?
8 In what year was NATO set up?
9 What is known as 'the Fourth Estate' in Britain?
10 What are the names of (a) the present Archbishop of Canterbury and (b) his predecessor?

3 *Geography*

1 Researchers maintain and believe that they can prove that Africa and South America were once one single land-mass. What proof have they?
2 Why are there hardly any important ports on the north coast of Russia?
3 In which direction does the south-west wind blow?
4 Why are hedges planted between fields in open country?
5 What is noticeable about the frontier between the USA and Canada?
6 Name the capitals of (a) the Netherlands and (b) Switzerland.
7 For what geographical feature is Greenwich famous?
8 Which European country has an exceptionally large number of lakes?
9 Which European country has an exceptionally large number of islands?
10 To which country or countries do the Mediterranean islands of (a) Sardinia and (b) Corsica belong?

4 *Biology*

1 In an emergency, how long can a healthy human being survive without (a) oxygen (b) liquid (c) solid food?
2 The vessels which take blood (a) to the heart and (b) from the heart are called . . . ?
3 What are rape seeds used for?
4 Certain body organs increase in size after being destroyed – e.g. by alcohol – not before. Which are they?
5 How many grams approximately does a blue-tit weigh?

6 What does UHT milk mean?
7 What is 'winter wheat'? (do not name types of wheat.)
8 Differences: 'Dappled' horses are grey. By what means are spotted greys and dappled greys distinguished? Why do we need the concept of 'spotted' and 'dappled' to help us?
9 What purpose important to life has human skin, apart from holding together, protection and covering?
10 Several essential functions are fulfilled by breathing through the nose: smell, warning, trapping dirt. What function is missing here?

5 *Physics/technology*

1 Water is boiling in two pots on the same fire. In pot A the water has been boiling for 10 seconds, in pot B it has been boiling for 100 seconds. In which pot is the water hotter?
2 To which natural science subject area do mechanics, optics and electricity belong?
3 How do you prevent thin wood from being split when putting in a nail?
4 What kinds of metal are soldered, and which welded? (Don't give names of metals, only types.)
5 What are rotating percussion drills used for? How do they work?
6 Where are the concepts 'concave' and 'convex' used; what do these terms mean?
7 Is the boiling point of water high on Mount Everest than it is in London?
8 When changing a wheel on a car, muscle power may not be sufficient to loosen a nut. How can you help yourself with the car's tool kit if even increasing the leverage by using an iron bar has no effect?

9 What law of physics forms the basis for thermometers?

10 What material or which elements are necessary for the formation of rust (apart from iron)?

6 *Mathematics*

In the areas of maths and geometry the candidate should know if special skills and knowledge are expected. Even if that is the case, these two sections should not be passed over.

The basic methods of writing down maths (plus, minus, multiplication, division) should be firmly fixed in the mind, including decimals. These form the basis for calculating, together with the use of brackets, raising to a higher power, finding the square root, fractions, and the conversion of one kind of measure into another. Pocket calculators are not allowed.

Knowledge cannot be picked up from here, only reinforced. If you need to, obtain help from a good arithmetic textbook or a friend with good knowledge of the subject.

Here is a little test to establish ability to do calculations:

1 $425.45+218.003-126.1+0.17-25\frac{3}{5}+8\frac{3}{8}=$
a) 500.982 b) 500.298 c) 500.289

2 $97.2\div12.15\times7.25=$
a) 58 b) 5.8 c) 60

3 $25+5\times10-40\div5+3-14\div7=$
a) 68 b) 5.86 c) 40.12

4 $26+(15-12\div4)+(5\times8-25\div5)-12\div6=$
a) 0.43 b) 15.6 c) 71

5 $\sqrt{144}+3^4-8^2\div4\div2+2^3=$

a) 93 b) 6.06 c) 28.125

6 $2\frac{1}{4}\times\frac{4}{27}\div\frac{4}{9}=$

a) $\frac{3}{4}$ b) $\frac{4}{27}$ c) $2\frac{1}{12}$

7 $3\frac{3}{4}+1\frac{2}{3}-2\frac{5}{6}=$

a) 2 b) $8\frac{1}{4}$ c) $2\frac{7}{12}$

8 $\frac{1}{8}$ t−1.2 dz+5000 g+4$\frac{3}{4}$ kg+4000 mg=

a) 14.754 kg b) 18.750 kg c) 187.500 kg

9 1$\frac{1}{4}$ m+3.5 dm+750 mm+125 cm+0.125 km=

a) 12.86 m b) 1286 m c) 128.60 m

Working out formulae:

10 levers: **P×a = Q×b** Find b

a) $b = \frac{P\times a}{Q}$ b) $b = \frac{P\times Q}{a}$ c) $b = \frac{Q\times b}{P}$

11 potential energy: **W = m×g×h** Find h

a) $h = \frac{m\times g}{W}$ b) $h = \frac{W}{m\times g}$ c) $h = \frac{W\times m}{g}$

12 kinetic energy: **W = ½ × m × v²** Find v

a) $v = \frac{m}{0.5\times W}$ b) $v = \sqrt{\frac{W}{0.5\times m}}$ c) v = ½×W×m

Putting related facts together (problem solving)

To solve these problems you need a knowledge of mathematical associations and how to decode them.

Mathematicians speak of 'decoding' and 'problem-solving strategies'. You can simply and straightforwardly say: which method of calculation will lead to the solution? You need to use knowledge of different ways of calculating.

- percentages
- calculation of interest
- working out invoices
- mixed problems
- division
- proportions
- establishing and checking time-spans
- calculating averages
- calculating scales
- using the rule of three
- equations
- the application of Pythagoras's theorem

1 A master craftsman calculates that he will need 9 employees to complete a job in 8 working days. The customer wants it completed in 6 working days. How many employees will have to be used?

a) 12 employees b) 14 employees c) 11 employees

2 A building trade foreman needs 880 litres of dry mortar made up of a mixture of sand: cement: lime = 18:3:1. Water used and loss of materials during mixing are not to be taken into account. How many litres of sand – cement – lime does he need?

a) 700 S, 100 C, 80L b) 680 S, 120 C 80 L
c) 720 S, 120 C, 40 L

3 A ladder 8.60m long is put on level ground 2.20m away from a right-angled house wall. How high will the ladder reach?

a) 8.25m b) 7.98m c) 8.31m

4 A contractor deducts 3% discount from an invoice and remits £2764.50. For what sum was the invoice made out?

a) £2847.40 b) £2850.00 c) £2845.50

5 A loan of £48000 is repayable after 2½ years with 8½% interest. What is the total amount to be repaid?

a) £59,400 b) £58,200 c) £61,200

6 A machine produces 4800 components per hour. Because of a breakdown the machine is idle for 15½ minutes. How many components are lost?

a) 1260 components
b) 1240 components
c) 1244 components

7 An iron merchant receives three types of hoop iron: 2.5 tons of type A, 4 tons of type B, and 2.6 tons of type C. The cost of transport comes to £455. What is the transport cost for each type?

a) £125, £200, £130
b) £110, £210, £135
c) £115, £205, £135

8 A recipe to serve 4 people says: 400 g flour, 50 g butter, 30 g sugar, 10 g spice. The cook has to bake for 15 people. What quantity of flour (F), butter (B), sugar (S) and spice (SP) is needed, rounded up/down to 10 g?

a) 1500 F, 190 B, 110 S, 40 SP
b) 1450 F, 200 B, 115 S, 45 SP
c) 1500 F, 180 B, 120 S, 40 SP

9 The following temperatures were recorded in one week at 7 a.m. Mon. 14°, Tues. 16.2°, Wed. 17.5°, Thurs. 15.9°, Fri. 16°, Sat. 15.1°, Sun. 15.9°. What was the average for the week?

a) 15.7° b) 15.8° c) 15.9°

10 The following is known about a cylindrical pillar:
$V = \pi \times r^2 \times h$ (formula for volume).
$V = 667.64cm^2$, $\pi=3.14$, $r=4.5cm$. How high is the pillar?

a) 10.5 cm b) 9.5 cm c) 10.0 cm

11 Three entrepreneurs invest a total of £60,000 in a business. A puts in £20,000, B puts in £15,000 and C puts in £25,000. The business does well – after a year it makes a profit of £15,000. How much does each get?

a) A £5,500 B £3,900 C £5,600
b) A £5,100 B £3,650 C £6,250
c) A £5,000 B £3,750 C £6,250

12 In drawing up a plan, the architect has forgotten to include the area of one room. The scale of the plan is 1:25. Measurement of the floor space of the room in sq.m is required. In the plan it is 13.8 cm long and 12.4 cm wide. The floor area measures:

a) 10.70 m^2 b) 17.11 m^2 c) 26.20 m^2

7 *Geometry*

This covers length (one-dimensional geometry), surfaces (two-dimensional geometry) and solids (three-dimensional geometry).

Anyone who can no longer remember the formulae for calculating:

- square
- right angle
- trapezoid
- parallelogram
- circle
- ellipse, etc.

and standard solids such as:

- cube
- square
- cylinder
- cone
- pyramid, etc.

should consult his or her old maths book (for nothing much has changed in this area) or a book of mathematical tables and data.

Finally, here are some typical geometry exercises.

1 Cubes with a length of a side of 4 cm have to be packed in a carton, the inside measurements of which are 24 × 20 × 16 cm. The cubes are to be packed close together so that the carton is packed tight. How many cubes will fit into the carton?

a) 80 cubes b) 120 cubes c) 160 cubes

2 A square room is 6400 m square. How long is each side of the square?

a) 64 m b) 80 m c) 32 m

3 A trapezoid has a base line of 18.0 cm. The upper, opposite side is 12.0 cm long. How long is the middle line?

a) 16 cm b) 15 cm c) 14 cm

4 In a parallelogram the sum of the angles is 360°. Angle A is 40°. How big is the opposite angle G?

a) 40° b) 60° c) 120°

5 An aluminium cone is 4.9 cm high. Its solid base has a diameter of 2.4 cm. Aluminium has a specific gravity of 2.69. How heavy is the aluminium cone?

a) 19.87 grams b) 11.76 grams c) 26.36 grams

6 The larger (outside) radius of a flat ring-shaped figure is ri = 2.3 cm. The smaller (inside) radius is r2 = 1.8 cm. What is the surface area of the ring in cm^2?

a) 6.44 cm^2 b) 4.14 cm^2 c) 8.20 cm^2

7 A pyramid has a square base the sides of which are 5.5 cm long. It is 30.0 cm high (not length of sloping sides). What is the volume of the pyramid in cm^3?

a) 302.5 cm^3 b) 300.0 cm^3 c) 330.25 cm^3

8 A round iron bar is 2.50m long and 25mm thick. The specific gravity of iron is 7.6. How many kg does the iron bar weigh?

a) 11.875 kg b) 4.750 kg c) 9.322 kg

8 *Spelling*

We cannot provide here a complete course on how to work on the correction of spelling mistakes. For that a book is necessary, one written specially with adult self-help in mind. Before you buy such a book it is a good idea to ask the advice of an experienced specialist, because almost every case of difficulty with spelling has a different cause.

Be careful about your choice – never buy on impulse! The size of a book says as little about its suitability as its price does. Besides, in case of doubt consult a good dictionary. The following list will serve merely as a preliminary investigation (an informal test) as to whether perhaps 'diagnosis and therapy' ought to follow.

Indicate the correct spelling for the following words:

1 a) generally
b) generely
c) generelly

2 a) acommodate
b) accomodate
c) accommodate

3 a) parralel
b) parallel
c) paralell

4 a) desicated
b) dessiccated
c) desiccated

5 a) ecstasy
b) ecstacy
c) eckstasy

6 a) embarrassment
b) embarassment
c) embarrasment

7 a) reciept
b) receipt
c) reseet

8 a) rythm
b) rhythm
c) ryhthm

9 a) benefiting
b) benifiting
c) benefitting

10 a) oprobium
b) opprobrium
c) approbrium

11 a) accessable
b) accessible
c) acksessable

12 a) irisistible
b) iresistable
c) irresistible

13 a) exercise
b) excersize
c) ecxersice

14 a) frend
b) friend
c) freind

15 a) bycicle
b) bicicle
c) bicycle

16 a) niece
b) kneece
c) neice

17 a) disgise
b) dizgize
c) disguise

18 a) pencilian
b) penicillin
c) pennycillian

19 a) consensus
b) concencus
c) concensus

20 a) duvcoat
b) dovecot
c) dovecote

21 a) aledged
b) alleged
c) aleged

22 a) alleygater
b) alligator
c) alegater

23 a) transister
b) transsistor
c) transistor

24 a) susceptible
b) susseptibul
c) susceptable

25 a) secretary
b) secetary
c) secretery

26 a) furniss
b) ferniss
c) furnace

27 a) cieling
b) ceiling
c) cealing

28 a) perswade
b) persuade
c) pursuade

29 a) alright
b) allright
c) all right

30 a) fulfil
b) fullfill
c) fullfil

Names

1 a) Febuary
b) Febuery
c) February

2 a) Thersday
b) Thurzday
c) Thursday

3 a) Sandwich
b) Sangwidge
c) Sandwitch

4 a) Middlesborough
b) Middlesbrough
c) Middlesborogh

5 a) Liecester
b) Leicester
c) Lesester

6 a) Missisippi
b) Misissipi
c) Mississippi

7 a) Batoven
b) Beetoven
c) Beethoven

8 a) Wagner
b) Wahgner
c) Vaagner

9 a) Piccasso
b) Picasso
c) Pickasso

10 a) Piccadilly
b) Picadilly
c) Picadily

11 a) Dackota
b) Dacoater
c) Dakota

12 a) Mackiaveli
b) Machiavelli
c) Macchiavelli

13 a) Canturbury
b) Cantuarbury
c) Canterbury

14 a) Gandhi
b) Ghandi
c) Ganhdi

15 a) Straights of Gibralter
b) Straights of Giballter
c) Straits of Gibraltar

More spellings:

1 a) accumulator
b) ackumulator
c) acumulator

2 a) appettite
b) apetight
c) appetite

3 a) arogants
b) arrowganse
c) arrogance

4 a) etticket
b) etiket
c) etiquette

5 a) ecksperteeze
b) xpertiese
c) expertise

6 a) thermomether
b) thermumether
c) thermometer

7 a) funeral
b) funerl
c) funerel

8 a) tollerence
b) tolerance
c) tolorance

9 a) disapearance
b) dissapearence
c) disappearance

10 a) asparagrass
b) asparregras
c) asparagus

11 a) temporary
b) temporery
c) temperery

12 a) sickosomatic
b) psycosommatic
c) psychosomatic

13 a) nitrogliceryn
b) nytroglisserin
c) nitroglycerin

14 a) carboreter
b) carberetter
c) carburettor

15 a) boardy
b) bordy
c) bawdy

Ambiguities

Here is a list of words. Fit the correct one by letter into the ten sentences below the list of letters. Note that not every word will be used and that it is possible that the same word fits more than one sentence.

a) peace
b) piece
c) popular
d) populous
e) grip
f) gripe
g) extant
h) extent
i) bass
j) base
k) lone
l) loan

1 He knew this was a . . . area but he had never seen so many small flats.
2 He knew this was a . . . area but he had never seen so many visitors.
3 To have shot a child was a truly . . . act.
4 His was the best . . . voice in the world.
5 She knew the colour of his hair but that was the . . . of her knowledge.
6 At last she felt calm and at . . .
7 Is the first folio of Hamlet still . . . ?
8 When things are bad it is useless to . . .
9 They were in the . . . of the fever.
10 He felt he needed a . . . of luck.

Answers

Intelligence section

PAGE	EXERCISE

page 8 Continuing a series of numbers

1	128	(×2×2×2 . . .)
2	40 320	(×2×3×4 . . .)
3	41	(+5−4×4+5 . . .)
4	56	(×4÷2+2×4 . . .)
5	204	(×3−1×3−1 . . .)
6	24	(+5+4−2+5 . . .)
7	132	(+2−7+10+2 . . .)
8	216	(×6÷2×6÷3×6÷2 . . .)
9	25	(÷5×10+15÷5 . . .)
10	130	(+1+2+4+8+16 . . .)

11

6	7	1	X	X	4	X	5	8	9

(×4÷2×4÷2 . . .)

12

X	4	X	4	3	7	6	5	X	9

(×3÷2×3÷2 . . .)

page 12 Happy families and odd-ones-out

Group:	possible generic term:
Cedar . . .	European conifers
Athens . . .	European capitals
Sycamore . . .	indigenous deciduous trees
Thames . . .	English rivers
Birmingham . . .	English cities
Crete . . .	European islands
pencil . . .	writing implements
water polo . . .	team ball-games
liver . . .	human organs
scooter . . .	two-wheeled vehicles

page 16 **Groups of five**

Group:	possible generic term:
oak . . .	indigenous deciduous trees
Volga . . .	non-British rivers
wheat . . .	indigenous grain crops
South Downs . . .	English hilly areas
cedar . . .	European conifers
fuel oil . . .	fuel/heating materials
Washington . . .	non-European capitals
cow . . .	farm animals
Severn . . .	English rivers
Vienna . . .	European capitals

page 17 **Groups of five/progressive sequences**

classification of the group according to:	first (or last) term in the group:
weight	gram
water course	spring
population	village
age	infant
speed	scooter
quantity/amount	seven
size	ant
sequence of vowels in the alphabet	a
source of income	beggar

page 18 **Outsiders (odd-one-out)**

Concept:	Basis:
1 stucco	not related to floor-covering
2 drink	not related to air
3 travel	not related to food
4 quite	not related to rain/water

5 cabbage	not related to school
6 harmless	heat and fire = danger
7 metal	not related to book
8 cat	not related to dog
9 work	concept group is holidays
10 see	concept group is telephone
11 lemon	not an indigenous fruit
12 tomato	not a root vegetable
13 tooth	concept group is to drink
14 travel	not related to senses
15 beach	not related to Christmas
16 harbour	concept group is road traffic/car
17 telephone	not radio/television
18 astonishing	not to see/hear
19 observe	concept group is letter
20 sparrow	not domestic animal

page 19 **Symbols** (odd-ones-out)

Symbol:	Basis:
1 c	triangle
2 e	overlapping
3 c	inside of circle is open
4 b	number of dots (here even number)
5 e	inner circles not on central axis
6 d	triangle not closed off in two places, open to the 'wings' on both sides
7 a	hair parting is on the man's left
8 e	10 spokes instead of 12
9 d	leaves alternate
10 d	the small shape does not turn the bigger shape into a quadrangle
11 c	thumb or small finger not shown
12 e	instead of increasing sizes, it has two rectangles of the same size
13 d	circle mixed with quadrangles

14 a	two strokes in a different direction
15 e	the longest arrow should be ahead of the others
16 a	there are 2 rounded and 2 right-angled pairs, but (a) is obtuse-angled
17 c	the other small circles are either on a straight line or at right angles to each other
18 e	except for e, each set contains 2 shapes with 1 dot and 2 shapes with 2 dots
19 b	the triangle lacks a dot
20 a	9 sides instead of 8

page 24 **Forming analogies**

1	1 fishbones	2 feathers	3 beak	4 humans
	5 birdcage	6 shell	7 cow, sheep	8 wages
2	1 darkness	2 drink	3 victory	4 car bicycle
	5 USA	6 pupil	7 son	8 nose
3	1 c)	2 b)	3 a)	4 d)
	5 d)	6 c)	7 b)	8 d)
4	1 d)	2 a)	3 d)	4 b)
	5 d)	6 a)	7 b)	8 c)

5 the basis for the analogy is in brackets
1 d) (no natural protection for the feet)
2 b) (protective clothing for work)
3 a) (equipment for work)
4 d) (superior authority at work)
5 d) (pact, treaties)
6 d) (directional steering)

7 c) (opposite sexes, male : female)
8 c) (country and county/state within that country)

6 the basis for the analogy is in brackets
1 d) (safety provision)
2 b) (place to stay overnight)
3 c) (fruit)
4 a) (content)
5 c) (the first material is produced from the second)
6 d) (cause and effect)
7 b) (cutting implement)
8 a) (one carries text, as the other carries sound)

7 the basis for the analogy is in brackets
1 d) (natural characteristics)
2 c) (long-term security)
3 a) (enclosing)
4 d) (remedy)
5 b) (perception)
6 c) (content)
7 b) (opposites)
8 d) (cause and – bad – effect)

8 Several answers can be meaningful and correct. Here are examples of answers that would be accepted as correct:
1 nicotine : tobacco = alcohol : brandy
2 fertilisation : life = accident : death/injury
3 bread : wheat = raisin : bunch of grapes
4 spoke : wheel = frame : reading-glasses
5 vinegar : acid = bacon : fat
6 chill : fever = short-circuit : fire
7 kilometre : distance = hour : time
8 skates : ice = roller skates : asphalt

page 30 **Logical consistency and sequency**

1 1) 6 2 1 3 4 5 2) 6 1 3 2 5 4
5 6 2 4 1 3
(roman numerals or letters of the alphabet)
3) 6 1 5 3 2 4 4) 6 3 5 2 1 4
5) 3 1 5 4 2 6 6) 6 2 4 3 5 1

2 1) 2 1 5 3 4 6 2) 3 2 6 4 5 1
3) 3 4 5 2 6 1 4) 1 3 4 6 2 5
5) 4 1 2 5 3 6 6) 4 6 3 2 1 5

In the case of 5 and 6 the reverse order of numbers in the answers is possible and equally correct.

3 Symbol:	Basis:
1 d)	1 – 2 – 3 – 4 – 5 circles
2 c)	adds a new shape
3 a)	odd numbers, decreasing
4 c)	increasing even numbers of petals, centre circle alternately open and filled in
5 a)	increasing each time by 45 degrees
6 a)	increase in the points from one, working from the upper segments to the lower, anti-clockwise
7 d)	the pattern of the pointer's movement is 90 degrees anti-clockwise
8 a)	the segments at the edge increase by one at 90 degrees anti-clockwise; the loops attached to the inner circle move at right angles clockwise; the dots in the centre circle increase by one

4 Symbol:	Basis:
1 c)	first symbol repeated in alternating position
2 b)	arrows increasing in size, alternately black and white
3 d)	alternating directions of diagonals, with an increase in the number of lines across them
4 c)	from one to three and back
5 a)	as 1 (c)
6 b)	the arrow is 90° farther on, anti-clockwise, with alternating point inside the circle
7 a)	taking the alternating open white circles, one line is added
8 d)	as 1 (c)

5 Symbol:	Basis:
1 b)	identical size to those on the left, but turned round
2 d)	continues the direction of the top of the triangle: below – right – left
3 c)	next stage towards completing the figure
4 a)	the shape on the right is moved to become the shape on the left
5 c)	a point is added alternately inside/outside, anti-clockwise
6 a)	the number of circles increases by one in panels 1 – 3 – 5; also the line at top right is in identical position in panels 1 – 3 – 5
7 b)	figure running in alternate directions, with fists clenched

8 a)	the centre circle is open in every second panel, and the number of black petals increases from one in panels 1 – 3 – 5

6 Symbols: Basis:

1 d)	increasing contents of container
2 a)	the line of the figures turns 45°; also the dot alternates from square to semi-circle
3 a)	diagonal strokes and dots increasing anti-clockwise
4 c)	alternately lighter and darker frames, black centre circles in white frames, inner lines in increasing odd numbers 1 – 3 – 5
5 d)	point with square beneath it in alternate positions, turning 90° anti-clockwise
6 d)	top right moving symbol appears finally at the bottom left
7 b)	increasing number of top row of dots, below alternating one or two black dots
8 d)	centre circles alternately white/black, the small inner lines increasing anti-clockwise

page 38 **Spatial concepts**

1 1 a – b – c – g   2 a – d – e – g
3 a – d – e – f   4 b – c – f – g
5 a – b – d – f   6 b – c – d – g

2 1a 2d 3b 4d 5b 6 all possible

3 1a b c 2a b d 3a c d 4a c d 5b c d 6a b c

Help in solving spatial problems

Exercise 3: Segments of geometric figures

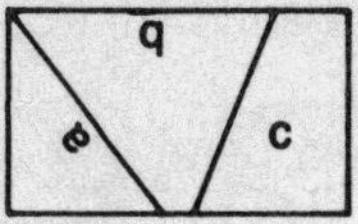

1 Answer: 1 a b c
The other way up is also possible

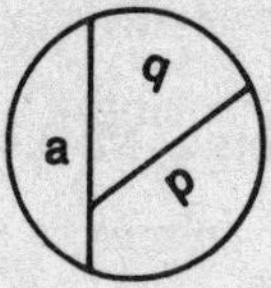

2 Answer: 2 a b d
could be turned, or put the other way up

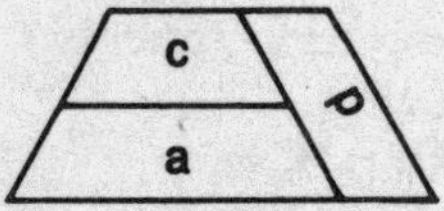

3 Answer: 3 a c d

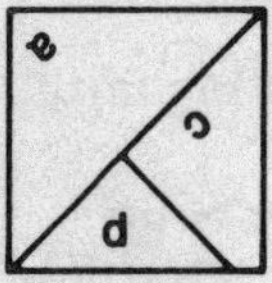

4 Answer: 4 a c d
could be turned, or put the other way up

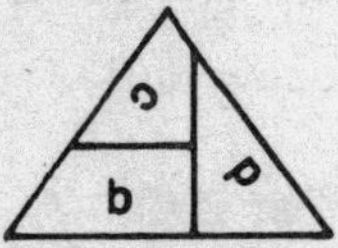

5 Answer: 5 b c d

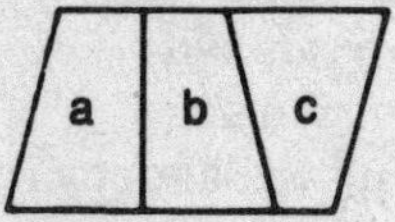

6 Answer: 6 a b c
The other way up is also possible

4 1 A1, B2, C4, D3, E2, F4, G1, H3, J1
2 A3, B3, C1, D2, E1, F2

5 1b 2a 3d 4d 5a 6c

6 1 1d – 2b – 3c and d – 4c – 5 none – 6a – 7 none – 8a
2 1c – 2 none – 3e – 4b – etc

page 57 **Ability to observe and remember**

1
1 Harry and Karen, George and Mary, Paul and Helen
2 Joan and Elizabeth with Karen, Alison with Mary
3 Edward with Harry, Gerald with George, Mark and Matthew with Paul
4 7 male, 7 female
5 7 people
6 7 tickets
7 Elizabeth
8 Gerald
9 Elizabeth, Mark and Gerald
10 nephews: Edward, Mark and Matthew
nieces: Joan and Elizabeth

2

1 right	2 no	3 no	4 no	5 six
6 24	7 seven	8 four	9 nine	10 four

3 Pattern of the flats:

1st floor left:
James Jordan
46 years old
engineer
Rita Jordan
42 years old
playgroup supervisor
2 sons

1st floor right:
Ian Sanderson
65 years old
pensioner
Pauline Sanderson
58 years old
no children

ground floor left:	ground floor right:
Ivor Williams	Stephen Foster
48 years old	58 years old
lawyer	shopkeeper
Edna Williams	Sarah Foster
46 years old	59 years old
teacher	bookkeeper
2 daughters	1 son, 2 daughters

1 Rita Jordan and Pauline Sanderson
2 Stephen Foster, James Jordan, Ian Sanderson
3 Three sons, four daughters
4 Sarah Foster, 59 years old
5 Teacher
6 100 years
7 Ivor Williams, 48 years old
8 Stephen Foster, Edna Williams, Sarah Foster
9 Rita Jordan, 42 years old and Ian Sanderson 65 years old
10 They do not exist

4 1a 2b 3a 4c 5b 6a 7b 8c 9a 10c 11c 12b

5 1c 2b 3b 4c 5a 6c 7c 8b 9a 10a

6 1c 2a 3c 4a 5a 6b 7c 8a 9a 10c

Section Relevant to Work

page 65 **Recognising symbols**

Evaluation in test conditions, with the template

1 You should have marked:

9	A	O	7	B	X	7	C	□
7	D		6	E	⊡	7	F	□
8	G		9	H	+			

2 You should have crossed out a total of 20 times:

5 6 9

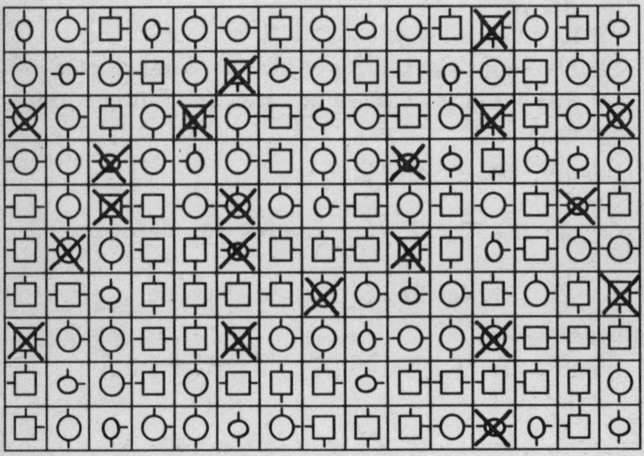

3 Each number should be marked 15 times.

1	2	3	4	5	6	7	8	9	0

1	5	8	2	8	6	0	9	2	1	8	4	6	6	3
3	6	7	4	0	4	7	6	4	3	8	7	3	5	4
7	1	0	1	9	5	1	7	7	4	1	3	5	2	3
6	9	8	7	8	2	7	0	2	5	2	3	1	2	2
9	8	5	2	4	6	4	1	7	1	8	0	7	5	7
1	5	2	1	3	8	0	2	3	2	0	2	3	3	5
2	5	4	8	0	6	8	6	5	3	9	5	6	9	1
7	1	1	3	5	3	9	4	9	4	9	4	0	6	4
6	2	5	9	6	9	9	9	6	8	6	0	1	0	8
8	3	8	7	0	0	7	4	4	0	9	7	9	5	0

page 68 **Mistakes in copying**

1 Total number of mistakes: 31
Errors in individual cases:

Greene: 4	Davison: 0	Greenberg: 5
Wyman: 3	Calder: 3	Miller: 3
Lancaster: 5	Tandy: 3*	Wood: 4*
Winter: 1		

*Counting town and county/district as 1.

	Model	Copy a	Copy b	Copy c
1	12051935	120519~~5~~5	12051~~8~~35	12051935
2	24101854	2410185~~2~~	24101854	24101854
3	30092010	300~~8~~2010	30092~~1~~10	300~~8~~20~~6~~~~1~~
4	15773346	1~~7~~~~5~~73346	15773346	157 73~~8~~46
5	20114612	2011~~8~~612	2011461~~1~~	20114612
6	37954231	3~~8~~954~~3~~~~2~~1	37~~5~~~~8~~4231	3795~~2~~~~4~~31
7	86686808	86~~8~~~~6~~~~8~~808	86686~~0~~~~8~~8	86686808
8	74437007	744370~~7~~~~0~~	7~~3~~437007	74437007
9	26996269	26~~8~~96269	269~~8~~62~~8~~~~9~~	269962~~8~~~~9~~
10	68698668	6~~8~~~~8~~9~~8~~~~8~~~~9~~8	68~~8~~9~~6~~~~8~~68	68698~~8~~68

	Original	Copy
1	B A 5 C 7 3 0 B	B A ~~8~~ ~~8~~ 7 3 0 B
2	X V u v x Z R S	X V u v x Z R S
3	8 8 6 8 6 8 8 6	~~8~~ ~~8~~ 6 8 6 8 ~~8~~ ~~6~~
4	S S Ƨ Я И R Ƨ Ɛ	S S Ƨ ~~R~~ ~~S~~ ~~N~~ Ƨ ~~E~~
5	○ □ X ⊠ ○ ○ □ ⊗	○ □ ~~⊠~~ ~~X~~ ○ ○ □ ⊗
6	└ ┐ ⊐ ⊓ └ ┘ ┌ ⊔	└ ┐ ~~⊏~~ ⊓ └ ┘ ┌ ⊔
7	C Ɔ ɑ V D C C ɑ	C Ɔ ~~D~~ V D ~~C~~ ~~C~~ ɑ
8	V ⊓ ⊔ Λ Λ ⊓ ⊓ ⊔	V ⊓ ⊔ ~~V~~ ~~V~~ ~~⊔~~ ~~⊔~~ ⊔
9	▯ ▯ ▭ ▭ ▯ □ ▯ □	▯ ▯ ▭ ▭ ▯ □ ~~□~~ □
10	8 3 ɛ 6 ə 6 8 6	8 3 ɛ ~~8~~ ~~6~~ ~~6~~ 8 6
11	ᒣ 5 ə ƨ ɛ 7 3 6	ᒣ ~~7~~ ~~8~~ ƨ ɛ 7 3 6
12	△ ◠ ▽ ◡ □ △ ◡ ◠	△ ◠ ▽ ◡ □ △ ◡ ◠
13	A A b c y A A A	A A ~~b~~ c y A A A
14	⊙ ○ ⊡ ○ ◕ ⁙ ◑ ○	⊙ ○ ⊡ ○ ~~◕~~ ~~⊡~~ ~~◑~~ ○
15	∀ ⋗ Λ ⋖ Λ < Λ ∀	∀ ⋗ Λ ⋖ Λ < ~~Λ~~ ~~∀~~

	Original	Copy
1	A i 3 6 V R 9 E	A i ~~Ɛ~~ ~~9~~ V R 9 ~~6~~
2	O X V 8 6 s K X	O X V ~~6~~ ~~8~~ s K X
3	⊓ ⊔ R S 8 T ⊥ O	⊓ ⊔ ~~Я~~ ~~Z~~ 8 T ⊥ O
4	S T O X □ ⊔ Λ U	S ~~⊥~~ O X ~~⊔~~ ~~□~~ Λ U
5	Q ⊔ X O + X O ⊓	Q ⊔ X ~~□~~ + X ~~□~~ ⊓
6	Ƨ S V Λ R T M N	Ƨ S V Λ R T M N
7	o J └ ┐ + U O ∩	o J ~~└~~ ~~┐~~ ~~X~~ U O ∩
8	A c B O a e U V	A ~~B~~ ~~c~~ O a e U V
9	W M N W N И И W	W M N ~~N~~ ~~W~~ ~~N~~ И W
10	6 9 0 8 3 ɛ ɘ ə	6 9 0 ~~3~~ ~~8~~ ɛ ɘ ə
11	m M n O P r S c	~~m~~ M ~~n~~ O P ~~r~~ S ~~c~~
12	□ △ ▽ ▽ □ ○ △ □	□ △ ~~△~~ ▽ ~~○~~ ○ △ □
13	V ⊔ W M N W M M	V ~~V~~ ~~M~~ M N W M M
14	8 7 6 5 9 i e u	8 ~~7~~ 6 ~~5~~ 9 i e u
15	0 8 o 6 9 8 8 6	0 8 o ~~6~~ ~~9~~ 8 8 ~~6~~

page 74 Putting letters in order

1 First letters

	H		
		T	
		B	
L			
			C
		I	
B			
		H	
	B		
		L	

S			
	P		
H			
	S		
	F		
			B
			C
		W	
			T
	B		

			N
			T
		W	
		W	
		F	
			C
B			
	C		
		R	
	M		

		S	
	W		
L			
			C
N			
		F	
L			
		R	
			B
		C	

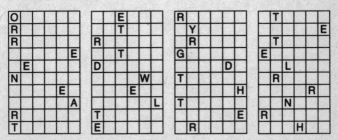

2 Middle letters

W				
				O
		O		
		L		
		N		
				I
			A	
	T			
		T		
		I		

				A
	R			
B				
			U	
		O		
P				
	S			
		I		
		A		
	A			

		E		
				B
	I			
G				
O				
U				
			A	
		A		
	E			
	E			

C				
		O		
				A
		M		
				N
	G			
				I
				A
O				
				E

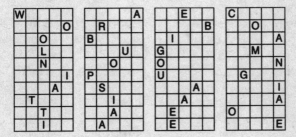

3 Last letters

O					
R					
R					
					E
	E				
N					
				E	
					A
R					
T					

		E			
		T			
R					
		T			
D					
				W	
			E		
					L
T					
E					

R					
	Y				
	R				
G					
				D	
T					
					H
T					
					E
	R				

	T				
					E
	T				
E					
		L			
	R				
				R	
		N			
R					
			H		

List of words for 'Putting letters in order'

1 **First letters:**

HIVE	SIDE	NOSE	STAG
TYRE	PAGE	TIME	WALL
BALL	HAND	WORD	LAMP
LAND	SACK	WEEK	CUBE
CHIN	FUEL	FACT	NAIL
IDEA	BATH	CREW	FORK
BODY	COAT	BAND	LEAF
HEAD	WIRE	CLAY	STAR
BIRD	TAPE	RICE	BEAD
LOAF	BOOK	MOTH	CARD

2 **Middle letters:**

TOWEL	CRACK	DRESS	UNCLE
GROUP	WORLD	ELBOW	FLOUR
FLOOR	TABLE	BRICK	SPADE
RULER	VAULT	LIGHT	WOMAN
MONEY	TOOTH	SPOON	TUNIC
DRINK	APPLE	MOUSE	TIGER
SCALP	MUSIC	GUARD	SHIRT
WATCH	KNIFE	PLANK	SNAIL
WATER	PLATE	SHEEP	BLOOD
ONION	CHALK	FIELD	BREAD

3 **Last letters:**

POTATO	GARAGE	WINTER	FOREST
CORNER	POCKET	CHERRY	ENGINE
MIRROR	FINGER	ANCHOR	INSECT
TONGUE	STREET	SPRING	COFFEE
SLEEVE	THREAD	WIZARD	BARREL

BUTTON	WINDOW	KNIGHT	COPPER
BRIDGE	KETTLE	CHURCH	SAUCER
BANANA	SHOVEL	TEAPOT	AUTUMN
HAMMER	CARROT	NETTLE	SILVER
PLANET	BLOUSE	SUMMER	BROOCH

page 76 **Doing calculations competently**

1 Estimating – rough calculation

1 a) 2340 2 b) 127 3 c) 800.80
4 a) 332¾ 5 d) 14800

Help with the answers:

For 1: As there are no brackets, the first thing to do is to calculate the products of 590×3 and 95×6. Both products have a nought in the unit position, as 3×0 = 0 and 6×5 = 30. When the products are added they can produce only a nought in the unit position – it is the same however large the products are – so the answer is: (a) 2340.

For 2: Division precedes addition, i.e. 24+3+100 = 127. Answer (b) 127.

For 3: Add only the figures after the points, thus: 25+50+05 = 80. The figures after the point can only be 80. Answer (c) 800.80.

For 4: Instead of calculating mixed figures (e.g. 112½), work out only the fractions (e.g. ½), thus: ½−¼+½ = ¾, i.e. answer (a) 332¾.

For 5: Work with only the tens, thus: 20−10+30−20+80 = 100. The result must be a complete hundred (two noughts at the end), so the answer is (d) 14800.

2 Using arithmetical short-cuts

1 a)	2 b)	3 b)	4 d)	5 a)
6 b)	7 d)	8 a)	9 c)	10 a)

Help with the answers:

For 1: Dividing by 3/multiplying by 3 as well as multiplying by 2/dividing by 2 cancel each other out to give 1. So the figures 24 remain as they are. Answer (a) 24.

For 2: The figures −/+ 168 and +/− 357 cancel each other out to give 0, leaving 698 (698 +/− 0 = 698). Answer 698.

For 3: Here it is a matter of division and multiplication only. Multiplying by nought (4th figure) gives nought – however high the figures in the calculation are up to that point. Any further result can only be nought. Answer: (b) 0.

For 4: It is tempting, of course, to calculate straight through from left to right, i.e. 4+6 = 10, then 10×2 = 20 and so on, but that is wrong. Keep in mind the rule 'multiply/divide before adding/subtracting', i.e. 4+12−2+6 = 20. Answer: 20.

For 5: $498 \div 498 = 1 \quad \sqrt{1} = 1 \quad \frac{17}{20-3} = \frac{17}{17} = 1$

i.e. 1×1×1 = 1, answer (a) 1.

For 6: You have to learn the knack of rapid calculation. It is relatively easy here because you have only to add up:
298+2 = 300, 145+55 = 200, 489+11 = 500. That gives 300+200+500 = 1000. Answer (b) 1000.

For 7: as for 6: 125+75 = 200, 63+37 = 100, 450+150 = 600. That gives 200+100+600 = 900. Answer (d) 900.

For 8: Similar to 6 and 7, but it isn't quite so straightforward. +225−175 = 50, +86−36 = 50, +200 is left, −77 is left. 50+50+200 = 300, 300−77 = 223. Answer (a) 223.

For 9: As this can be solved in any order, the following method seems logical, in order to avoid having too large intermediate results to handle: 4÷2 = 2, 9÷3 = 3, from which 2×3 = 6 and 6×7 = 42 become possible. Answer (c) 42.

For 10: Similar to 9, though somewhat less obvious: 4÷2 = 2 (must later be multiplied by 2), 25÷5 = 5 (then 5×11). That gives as a mental arithmetic calculation 5×11 (=55)×2 = 110. Answer (a) 110.

3 Stamina

a) 3	b) 21	c) 30	d) 38	e) 50
f) 18	g) 3	h) 28	i) 5	j) 16
k) 6	l) 20	m) 7	n) 50	o) 60

Stamina – Exercise A

16	6	8	14	63	56	90	18	81	4
22	7	14	18	56	64	81	16	64	3
30	4	10	13	49	72	72	17	49	5
16	3	6	12	35	48	81	15	64	6

Stamina – Exercise B

3	24	3	10	40	88	20	24	76	9
6	8	12	8	20	28	19	54	31	18
10	9	4	16	40	8	19	39	95	18
15	12	1	4	24	38	17	49	20	27

4 Being systematic

Vertically from top to bottom:
12/17/31/30/21/20/26/15/25/25/22/21
17/28/30/20/22/16/20/24/10/26/24/25/23
Total 550

Horizontally from left to right:
140/126/143/141
Total 550

It is quicker this way:

$$
\begin{aligned}
5 \times 1 &= 5\\
10 \times 2 &= 20\\
10 \times 3 &= 30\\
15 \times 4 &= 60\\
10 \times 5 &= 50\\
10 \times 6 &= 60\\
10 \times 7 &= 70\\
15 \times 8 &= 120\\
15 \times 9 &= 135\\
\hline
\text{Total} & \quad 550
\end{aligned}
$$

5 Being practical

4+8=32	64−8=8	72÷9=81	54÷6=60	48÷8=56
16÷8=24	7×2=5	15÷5=20	5×4=1	8+1=8
5+9=45	8×4=4	3+9=27	7×1=6	4×2=2
27−9=3	2+7=14	5×4=1	6+6=36	8×7=1
9×5=4	15×3=18	5+7=35	49−7=7	20÷5=5
12÷6=18	18−2=9	6×2=4	10÷=15	8+8=64
6+6=36	35÷7=42	36−6=6	27−3=9	6+6=36
9−3=3	8+8=64	16÷2=18	2+7=14	8×3=5
3+8=24	80÷8=88	5×1=4	45−5=9	15−5=3
10×9=1	25−5=5	9+6=54	27÷3=30	8×7=1
35÷5=40	16÷4=20	36−9=4	16−4=4	1+9=9
5+7=35	8×7=1	21÷3=24	9×6=3	12÷3=15
64÷8=72	28÷4=32	5+5=25	9+3=27	7×4=3
72÷9=81	10+9=90	36÷4=40	9×8=1	21÷7=28
5+5=25	6×3=3	10×3=7	30÷5=35	81−9=9

Finding solutions and solving problems:

1 0   2 120   3 9   4 1   5 all
6 24   7 140   8 52   9 a) never   b) 47 days
10 The cashier has no £5 or £10 notes.

page 92 Accuracy and organisation

1 Clock faces: evaluate these under test conditions by using a template.
2 Circle in squares, as before, using a template.
3 Circles, squares and crosses, as before, using a template.

1	8	4	6	0	7	7	8	3	3	0	0	7	1	1	2
2	1	4	1	8	2	0	7	3	8	3	0	2	8	4	4
3	0	6	0	8	2	0	8	1	3	0	8	0	0	3	0
4	4	0	9	2	3	8	0	7	0	7	6	2	4	1	7
5	1	2	2	7	0	8	0	9	0	6	9	2	2	6	0
6	4	3	6	0	4	8	0	1	8	0	8	6	0	4	0
7	1	6	2	3	1	4	8	9	2	1	7	9	1	0	9
8	0	4	6	7	3	0	6	9	7	8	8	9	+	1	4
9	9	4	6	9	8	8	0	2	6	6	1	9	9	3	3
10	1	3	8	0	4	1	2	9	8	7	3	0	8	0	1
11	8	5	0	9	7	3	6	0	9	3	1	1	9	8	8
12	+	9	9	1	7	8	8	5	7	2	6	7	9	9	0
13	2	3	0	4	7	8	9	4	9	0	8	0	9	1	8
14	8	0	4	3	7	7	0	7	0	3	1	6	9	7	+
15	9	1	7	9	6	6	9	0	3	9	9	9	9	1	9
16	8	4	2	7	8	0	8	+	3	6	1	9	8	9	8
17	0	4	6	9	7	7	7	9	2	6	0	3	9	0	2
18	8	8	8	0	1	9	1	3	7	7	0	7	7	1	0
19	4	0	2	6	3	0	0	8	8	7	6	9	8	7	9

page 97 **Organisation**
1

1st Task Alphabet	2nd Task Turnover in order		3rd Task Discount in order	
Name	Name	Turnover	Name	Discount
Madden	Madle	500,000	Madrugo	765
Maddox	Madison	300,000	Madden	750
Maddy	Madhani	250,000	Madewell	700
Madely	Magee	150,000	Magilton	675
Madewell	Magilner	125,000	Magness	600
Madgett	Maddox	100,000	Madgett	560
Madgwick	Magley	95,000	Magill	540
Madhani	Magill	90,000	Magnet	525
Madison	Madrugo	85,000	Madeley	500
Madistore	Madistone	80,000	Maggs	480
Madle	Magness	75,000	Magley	475
Madrugo	Madgett	70,000	Magee	450
Magee	Madgwick	60,000	Maddy	420
Maggs	Madeley	50,000	Madistone	400
Magill	Magilton	45,000	Magilner	375
Magilner	Maddy	35,000	Madgwick	360
Magilton	Maggs	30,000	Maddox	300
Magley	Madden	25,000	Madhani	250
Magness	Madewell	20,000	Madison	240
Magnet	Magnet	15,000	Madle	100
	4th Task	220,000	5th Task	9,465

2 Possible weekly timetable
(other alternatives possible and correct)

Shift	Mon.	Tue.	Wed.	Thur.	Fri.	Sat.	Sun.
Early	John	John	Henry	Henry	Derek	Derek	Arnold
Late	Albert	Albert	Harry	Harry	Maurice	Maurice	Charlie
Night	Ken	Ken	Sam	Sam	Arnold	Frank	Frank

page 101 **Technical understanding**

1 C	2 B	3 C	4 B	5 B
6 C	7 C	8 C	9 B	10 B
11 A	12 B	13 C	14 A	15 B

General knowledge and school subjects

page 108 General knowledge

1 Eight 2 Criteria 3 Three
4 Five rings, one for each continent
5 Historical example from the age of chivalry : adjusting the visor on armour before/after combat
6 In case of emergency: it can be reached by the front seat passenger
7 By vaporisation
8 Alpha and omega are the first/last letters of the Greek alphabet
9 The masts are laid flat and when ship is in the bottle they are pulled upright by a thread which is then removed
10 ® means 'registered'; the trademark is therefore protected

page 108 History/politics

1 a) England, Scotland, Wales
b) England, Scotland, Wales and Northern Ireland
2 a) Mary b) George VI
3 Tombs for the pharoahs/kings, approx. 5000 years ago
4 Jesus (Iesus) of Nazareth, King (rex) of the Jews (Iudorum)
5 St George (red on white), St Andrew (diagonal, white on blue), St Patrick (diagonal, red on white)
6 a) 1066 b) 1805
7 1917
8 1949
9 The Press
10 a) George Carey b) Robert Runcie

page 109 **Geography**

1 Coastal outline (shape), rocks, fauna, flora
2 Free of ice for only a short time
3 From the south-west to the north-east
4 As wind-breaks and to prevent soil erosion
5 Horizontal line (no natural frontier)
6 a) Seat of government: The Hague; main city: Amsterdam b) Bern(e)
7 The Greenwich maridian (imaginary north-south line on the earth's surface between the north and south poles, taken to be 0° longitude) passes through it
8 Finland
9 Greece
10 a) Italy b) France

page 109 **Biology**

1 a) 3 minutes b) c. 3 days c) c. 30 days
2 a) veins b) arteries
3 To extract their oil content
4 Liver (cirrhosis), brain
5 c. 8-12 grams
6 Ultra-heat treated (sterilised for longer keeping)
7 Sown in autumn, it grows through the winter
8 Size of the dark (grey) markings
spotted greys=grey markings, small, like spots/flecks
dappled greys=grey markings, large, like apples
9 Breathing
10 Warming cold air

page 110 **Physics/technology**

1 The temperature is the same
2 Physics
3 Knock the point of the nail flat
4 Soft metal: solder
Hard metal: weld
5 Concrete and rock. Rotating percussion drills bore and hammer at the same time
6 In physics/optics, in lenses: curved inwards=concave; curved outwards=convex
7 No, the other way round
8 Apply the spider spanner so that one arm points more or less horizontally to the right. Lift this arm by jacking it up. The nut will loosen
9 Expansion by warming
10 Water (H_2O, hydrogen, and oxygen)

page 111 **Mathematics**

Informal test:

1 b)	2 a)	3 a)	4 c)	5 a)	6 a)
7 c)	8 a)	9 c)	10 a)	11 b)	12 b)

Putting related facts together (problem solving)

1 a)	2 c)	3 c)	4 b)	5 b)	6 b)
7 a)	8 a)	9 b)	10 a)	11 c)	12 a)

page 116 **Geometry**

1 b)	2 b)	3 b)	4 a)
5 a)	6 a)	7 a)	8 c)

page 118 **Spelling**

1 a)	2 c)	3 b)	4 c)	5 a)
6 a)	7 b)	8 b)	9 a)	10 b)
11 b)	12 c)	13 a)	14 b)	15 c)
16 a)	17 c)	18 b)	19 a)	20 c)
21 b)	22 b)	23 c)	24 a)	25 a)
26 c)	27 b)	28 b)	29 c)	30 a)

Names

1 c)	2 c)	3 a)	4 b)	5 b)
6 c)	7 c)	8 a)	9 b)	10 a)
11 c)	12 b)	13 c)	14 a)	15 c)

More spelling:

1 a)	2 c)	3 c)	4 c)	5 c)
6 c)	7 a)	8 b)	9 c)	10 c)
11 a)	12 c)	13 c)	14 c)	15 c)

Ambiguities

d c j i h a g f e b